BLAKE AND MILTON

BLAKE

AND

MILTON

BY

DENIS SAURAT

New York
RUSSELL & RUSSELL
1965

FIRST PUBLISHED IN 1935
REISSUED, 1965, BY RUSSELL & RUSSELL, INC.
BY ARRANGEMENT WITH GEORGE ALLEN & UNWIN, LTD., LONDON
L.C. CATALOG CARD NO: 65—18830
PRINTED IN THE UNITED STATES OF AMERICA

1319997

CONTENTS

INTRODUCTION

THERE is a peculiar relationship between Blake and Milton. We find in them many similar qualities; many fundamental ideas are held in common by both. But in Blake the Miltonic characters are distorted. Or, if we prefer to call it so, transfigured; as though Milton were a clear-cut and normally built original, and Blake a sort of reflection in one of those transforming mirrors which change the shape and the proportions of the objects they picture.

Blake is a wild brother of Milton; it might be said a Milton gone mad, had not that word "mad" too ominous a ring when used in connection with Blake; but anyhow a Milton who has broken the bonds of self-control and all control, and allows his magnificent soul to pour itself out haphazard, without aim or rule, according to a sort of magnanimous and careless capriciousness.

We shall find in both much the same elements and impulses, but, in Milton, majestically regulated and marching in grand array; in Blake, running riot and too often fighting among themselves.

7

One fundamental principle is clear in the study of the relationship between the two poets. For both, as we shall see, the elemental parts of human life are passion and reason; but in Milton reason rules over desire, while Blake's aim is to set passion free from all control of reason.

With this key, one can, more or less approximately, translate Milton's career and ideas into Blake's.

There is, of course, first of all, a direct influence of Milton over Blake; Milton was Blake's idea of a great poet; Blake had passionately studied the works of his predecessor, and had illustrated *Paradise Lost.* Therefore he draws many of his conceptions directly from Milton. But probably even a larger part of his ideas are elaborated out of Milton's, often by combating Milton's. Milton's ideas are data for Blake's mind which Blake uses as intellectual food, partly assimilates, partly transforms nearly past recognition, and partly rejects.

It is, further, a curious fact that many of Milton's ideas, not known to Blake, and revealed to the world in the *Treatise of Christian Doctrine* when Blake's days of song were over[1], are yet quite

[1] In 1825. Blake died in 1827, but his last important work, *The Everlasting Gospel* was written about 1810.

similar to many conceptions of the visionary mystic.

More than anything else, this shows the deep relationship extant between the two poets' minds and characters.

More than in direct or indirect influence, the source of all resemblances is in the remarkable similarity of mind and temperament: the one exception, Blake's lack of self-control, being the spring of most of the differences; and the different circumstances modifying the garb rather than the essentials.

We shall therefore study first the characters of the two poets in their similar traits, and add to that what we know of the direct influence of the study of Milton upon Blake.

In a second part, we shall try to parallel their central conceptions of life, as regards the relation of passion to reason; whence proceed both similarities and differences in the political and moral conception of liberty; and, related thereto, in the ideas on the Fall and the Regeneration of Man, and more particularly on sex questions.

In a third part, we shall deal with the resemblances in the two poets' general metaphysical outlook, and particularly in their way of dealing with dogma or myth.

We shall thus have traced, as much as we can, the influence of the similar constitution of mind and temper on the psychological and moral views, on the one hand, and on the metaphysical ideas on the other.

This study is not only interesting as throwing light on many of Blake's characteristics by the help of better-known and similar traits in Milton; it is a great help also to the Miltonic student. Very many feelings and ideas exist in Milton in a latent state, owing to the repression put upon them by his self-control, or to the peculiar circumstances of his career or period. We find those germs fully developed in Blake, quite unrestrained by his own will and very little influenced by his period.

Thus very often the study of Blake is like a magnifying glass held over many important peculiarities of Milton.

A better understanding of both poets in their philosophical position is the aim of this study of the relationship between Blake and Milton.

CHAPTER I

LIFE AND CHARACTER

FIRST of all, and this is perhaps the most important point, Blake and Milton are compeers in spiritual pride.

With both, the trait is manifest already in childhood. Milton was deliberately brought up as a future great man, and kept through his whole life this early habit of considering himself as one.

Blake, having received a flogging from his father at seven years of age for reporting one of his early visions—which was, naturally enough, taken as a lie—wrote in Tiriel, some twenty-five years after:

The father forms a whip to rouse the sluggish senses
    to act
And scourges off all youthful fancies from the new-
    born man.

"His feeling of personal dignity," writes Mr. E. J. Ellis[1], "was, next to the love of art and vision, the ruling passion of his life. He long disliked the

---

[1] *The Real Blake*, p. 5.

very word 'father.' It is often a term of reproach
in his poems. He was intensely affectionate, but
held as a fixed rule that he must be neither con-
trolled nor criticised. His pride, like his genius,
was beyond all ordinary measure, and grew with
his growth."

The word "pride" is perhaps too narrow. With
both poets, pride was only one of the manifestations of a powerful egotism, which, more or less
consciously, ruled their whole lives.

One of the characteristic forms of that egotism
in both is their intense partisanship and fierce
aggressiveness on occasion. No man could be more
bitter than Milton against political or religious
enemies about whom he really knew hardly anything, unless it be Blake passing strictures on artists
of whose works he was largely ignorant[1]; and none
had at his command more foul or virulent language
against his foes than Milton, or than Blake against
his offending friends. It takes all the ingenuity of
commentators to discover the purely moral offence
of Hayley's which Blake stigmatizes thus:

And when he could not act upon my wife
Hired a villain to bereave my life."

[1] He chiefly knew the works of Rembrandt, Titian, etc., whom he
criticises so bitterly on principle, from prints and reproductions.

The same pride and self-assertiveness is manifested by the two poets in the world of spirits in
which they so largely live and move. In the midst
of his gigantic and terrifying chaos of angry phan-
toms, Blake remains calm and master of himself.
Such intense and appalling visions as his should
probably have ended in veritable madness, had he
not possessed a truly formidable power of self-
assertion, which enabled him to treat the terrific
spirits as his equals and even as his inferiors, and
kept terror down in his heart. Just as a visionary
monk of the middle ages could only resist the
devils he saw by being conscious of a higher power,
the power of God, sustaining him, so Blake's moral
and intellectual forces can only have been preserved
by his consciousness of the same higher power,
although only in his own personality.

In a letter to Thomas Butts, Blake describes in
verse his contention against the terrible spirits:

> With silver angels across my way,
> And golden demons that none can stay.
> With my father hovering on the wind,
> And my brother Robert just behind,
> And my brother John, the evil one,
> In a black cloud making his moan.
> Tho' dead, they appear upon my path.
> .   .   .   .

Then Los appeared in all his power,
In the sun he appeared, descending before
My face in fierce flames.

And Blake faces Los, and tells him:

"Thou measurest not the time to me,
Nor yet the space that I do see;
My mind is not with thy light array'd
Thy terrors shall not make me afraid."
When I had my defiance given,
The sun stood trembling in his Heaven.

Another such encounter is described in *Milton:*

While Los heard indistinct in fear, what time I bound
    my sandals
On: to walk forward through Eternity, Los descended
    to me;
And Los behind me stood; a terrible flaming sun: just
    close
Behind my back: I turned round in Terror, and behold
Los stood in that fierce glowing fire; and he also stood
    down
And bound my sandals in in Udan-Adan; trembling
    I stood
Exceedingly with fear and terror, standing in the vale
Of Lambeth: but he kissed me and wished me health
And I became One Man with him arising in my
    strength:

'Twas too late now to recede : Los had entered into my
    soul
His terrors now possess'd me whole, I arose in fury and
    strength.[1]

And neither Blake nor Milton, in spite of their deeply religious spirit,

> Lean on our fair father Christ.

Blake never calls the Redeemer to help him in his struggles; Milton, who in theory, had a greater belief in Christ's Mission, in fact does not rely upon Him, and is quite content with the Heavenly Muse's company in his perilous travels through the abyss.

For Milton also had his strength in himself. He fears the Evil Spirits even less than Blake. Terror and trembling, which are such features of Dante's *Inferno*, are absent from *Paradise Lost*. Dante was protected, and the sense of protection does not prevent fear, for the question remains to the anxious soul, "What if protection be withdrawn?" But Milton had no need of protection. He faced Satan alone and fearlessly. He describes his terrible and magnificent demons with an impetuous fierceness of criticism which springs

[1] *Milton*, p. 19.

from the consciousness of his own superiority to
them. He reminds them constantly, in and out of
season, that they are only rebellious devils, that
for all their strength and grandeur, they are only
heaping on themselves

Treble confusion, wrath and vengeance poured.

Indeed it is only this deeply felt superiority of his
which enables Milton to sympathize in a measure
with his Fiends: which he could not do if he feared
them.

Both in Milton and Blake then there is the same
high-spirited attitude in their exploration of the
unknown world. And for both this intense self-
consciousness ends in making the poet the real
hero of the poem.

The splendid lyrical passages of *Paradise Lost*
have a deep significance. They represent to us
Milton in the different stages of his dangerous
undertaking. He prays to the Spirit:

What in me is dark,
Illumine, what is low, raise and support;[1]

He rejoices over his escape from

[1] *Paradise Lost*, I, 22.

> The Stygian pool, though long detained
> In that obscure sojourn—
> Taught by the Heavenly Muse to venture down
> The dark descent, and up to re-ascend,
> Though hard and rare.[1]

to "revisit safe" the Holy Light of his search.

It is because, in his spirit, he has confronted the great adversary. He emerges at times from the great struggle, to pray and sing in his own name. But all through the Satanic parts of his poem, Milton himself fights the Foe. There is in *Paradise Lost* a greater character than Satan: there is one who follows the Rebel unceasingly, unmercifully, in all his enterprises, showing him up at every step, branding his speeches and his exploits with a red bitterness of invective, holding up and shaking "the Infernal Serpent" before our astonished eyes: and it is not God, or Messiah: it is Milton who is the conqueror of Satan, and the veritable hero or *Paradise Lost*.

And in the same way, Blake is the hero of his *Prophetic Books*, the one character in them we do really know anything about.

> If only philosophy could find it out,

---

[1] *Paradise Lost*, III, 14, 19.

and philosophy has tried hard, all the terrible Shades of the Prophecies, Urizen and Los, and *Vala* and *Enitharmon* are only expressions of parts of Blake's mind and thought; and the subject of all his poems is the description of the passionate conflicts raging perpetually in his own wild and populous soul.

Like Milton, and more openly and naively, Blake has made his own private experience the fuel of his "Intellectual Furnaces." He promoted the coarse and brutal soldier Schofield, who had a tussle with him in the Felpham garden, to the rank of Son of Albion[1]; and his gentle wife, Catherine, is possibly responsible for the erratic behaviour of all the "Emanations."

Thus the final incarnation of Los and of Milton in Blake himself, who declares boldly speaking as Los:

> "I am that Shadowy prophet,
>   Who, six thousand years ago,
>   Fell from my station in the
>   Eternal Bosom."[2]

is only the revelation of the fact of Blake's presence all through the *Prophetic Books*.

[1] In *Jerusalem*.
[2] *Milton*, p. 20, 1, 15.

Both Milton and Blake had the same belief that they, in common with all poets, were divinely inspired. Blake said of *Jerusalem:*

"I have written this poem from immediate dictation; the authors are in eternity."[1]

And Milton's widow declared, on his behalf:

"He stole from nobody but the Muse that inspired him, and that was God's Holy Spirit."[2]

But both went further, and thought themselves not only inspired of God, but actually parts of the Divine Being Himself.[3]

This pantheistic attitude of mind is quite in keeping with the exalted idea they had of themselves; the philosophical theory worked with especial effectiveness when applied to their own powers and role as prophets in the world.

But there was nothing meanly selfish and narrow-minded about either of them. However great their appreciation of themselves, both admitted, in theory at least, the whole of mankind to the high privileges they claimed personally. Both were too intensely preoccupied with their own minds to see clearly that all men were not as they; and they made their own experience and law the rule of the universe of men, and of the Universal

---

[1] Letter to Butts.
[2] Masson, VI, 746.
[3] Cf. p. 127 and p. 144 of this study.

Mind. It is thus their generosity of soul, joining with their personal pride, which drove them to claim for Man the highest standard of Being, and participation in the Divine Being. Their Pantheism was an intellectual transposition of their characters.

This principle of pride in both thinkers had the most direct and far-reaching effect on their thought: and it worked in similar ways. Thus both were led to justify the desires and instincts they felt living in themselves: and similar systems of morality sprang from that need, similar in spite of differences essential also.

This justification of the natural instincts of man led them both to suppress the usual distinction between body and soul; and both proclaimed the unity of the human being, with only differences of degree between bodily and spiritual powers.

Lastly, the imperious need of their pride was liberty. And both extended to the whole of mankind in all its activities the benefit of that privilege.

Thus similarities in their politics, in their ethics and in their metaphysics are traceable to this similarity of pride in their very spiritual constitution.

A second great trait common to both poets is their intense and, at bottom, physical, susceptibility

to feminine influence. Both were rather short
men, but of vigorous frame and ardent temperament; both enjoyed good health and strength
through a long life. In both, physical passion lay
dormant but powerful and ready to break forth.

Both entered into the life of passion with a shock
which had great influence on their views of women
and of life.

Milton found himself wedded to a "dull and
spiritless mate" who abandoned him after a few
weeks of unmarried life, and the pent-up passion,
first roused and then thwarted in him is like a
powerful undercurrent in the divorce pamphlets.

Blake threw himself heart and soul into his first
love, and was similarly baffled, and called "a fool,"
for all his eloquence, by Polly Woods.[1]

Mr. Ellis writes, in words which apply to Milton's case at least as well as to Blake's:

"The shock was a severe one. Blake's temperament being ardent, his character confident, and his
heart affectionate and trustful, the whole woof and
warp of his emotional fabric was torn to scraps at
once. Love, self-regard and hope were wounded.
A fit of extreme wretchedness came upon him."

It is characteristic also of both men that both
betook themselves to more favourable deities,

[1] Ellis, *The Real Blake*, p. 37-38.   Mona Wilson, *Life*, p. 27.

Milton without any serious consequences, but Blake to find his true companion.

But even Blake's marriage did not run smooth at the first; and domestic trouble of a kind similar to Milton's attended the beginning of his married life.

It has been asserted that Milton's marriage was purely a nominal one, during the honeymoon from which his bride fled.[1] Hence Milton's curious preoccupation in the divorce pamphlets with the means that curb the flesh, such as strict diet and exercise.[2]

Mr. Ellis seems to have revealed a similar passage in Blake's life: "the blow of blighting censorious contempt"[3] of the society her husband brought her into, made Catherine Blake shrink back to the ideal of her Puritan youth.

"She alienated by rebuke the husband whose love she had won by pity first and by pleasure after."

And then it was probably, or perhaps in remembrance of that time, that Blake wrote *William Bond:*

[1] Cf. Pattison, Sir Walter Raleigh, etc.

[2] *Doctrine and Discipline of Divorce* (Bohn), p. 194 et 205 (See: *Milton, Man and Thinker*, p. 49, et seq.)

[3] Ellis, *The Real Blake*, p. 89-90. This is, however, somewhat hypothetical.

"I wonder whether the girls are mad,
And I wonder whether they mean to kill,
And I wonder if Willian Bond will die,
For assuredly he is very ill."

And in this case again, the same experience led the two poets to the same thought: both went over to the cause of polygamy, and retained that ideal to the end of their lives.

Crabb Robinson is frightened into German and reports of Blake:

"He says that from the Bible he has learned that *eine Gemeinschaft der Frauen statt finden sollte.*"[1]

Milton devotes pages of his *Treatise on Christian Doctrine* to proving the lawfulness of polygamy.[2]

But when it came to practical action, both Blake and Milton were stopped by the same feeling of human kindness. Blake gave way before his wife's tears; and Milton received Mary Powell into his home again.

Both left us poetical presentations of either scene, Blake in *William Bond:*

Mary trembled and Mary chilled
And Mary fell down on the right hand floor,
That William Bond and his sister Jane
Scarce could recover Mary more.

[1] *Crabb Robinson's Diary*, Symons' edition, p. 269.
[2] *Treatise of Christian Doctrine*, p. 225 to 237.

When Mary woke and found her laid
On the right hand of her William dear,
On the right hand of his loved bed,
And saw her William Bond so near,
The Fairies that fled from William Bond
Danced round her shining head—

And Milton in the more famous scene of
Paradise Lost[1]:

She ended weeping and her lowly plight
Immoveable till peace obtained from fault
Acknowledged and deplored, in Adam wrought
Commiseration; soon his heart relented
Towards her, his life so late and sole delight,
Now at his feet submissive in distress;
Creature so fair his reconcilement seeking—

It was impossible for both poets to keep
their lives out of their poems, the veil covering the
autobiography being but of the thinnest in either
case.

These experiences made both poets give a
similarly large part in their work to the subject of
sensuality; their ideas of the Fall centred round
that point, and both alternately justified and condemned sensual passion, according to circumstance,
mood or principle.

[1] X, 937.

It is also remarkable—as against this fact of the place taken by sensuality in their poetry—that love proper, and sentimentality, appear but very little in their song. Neither Blake nor Milton are amatory poets.[1] The question of sensuality was to them a burning problem; but they generally avoided or ignored the subject of love, of which both had the highest ideal.

Milton knew the approach of loveliness:

> Authority and reason on her wait,
> As one intended first, not after made,
> Occasionally, and to consummate all,
> Greatness of mind and nobleness their seat
> Build in her loveliest, and create an awe
> About her, as a guard angelic placed.[2]

And that ideal of the union of man and woman in spirit and intelligence as well as in passion, which Milton analyses and demands in the Divorce tracts, Blake[3] realized fully in his life with Catherine, whom he taught to draw and to engrave and to see visions and to understand and believe in him.

In both poets there was the same disinclination

[1] Cf. Berger, *William Blake, poet and mystic*, p. 239-240.
[2] VIII, 555.
[3] See below, p. 114.

to "sing out their hearts." For both were proud and fastidious men; both kept themselves clean and faithful to the chosen wife through life, in spite of theories, just as both had led a pure youth; because of an instinct of purity in them, which would not let them contaminate their bodies or their souls. This delicacy of pride made of them both staid family-men. It shows the more the resemblance of their moral constitution, that whereas Milton in his chastity realized his ideal, Blake's wild glorification of lust tallies not at all with his own behaviour. In spite of different principles, the moral conduct was the same.

The third great common character in the life and work of the two poets comes from what may be called their spiritual attitude.

Both have an intense religious spirit, fostered by their early education and home environment. Both were fed intellectually on the Bible from their infancy, both grew up in an atmosphere of opposition to the prevalent religious current of their time: Milton among the Puritans, Blake under a Swedenborgian father.

Thus not only were both filled with intense religious feeling, but, in spite of that, and also through that, both were great enemies of religion: thorough-going individualists and heretics, impatient of all discipline, contemners of all known dogmas, bitter opponents of all priests and churches.

For the spirit in them was not religious only; it was also, it was perhaps chiefly, intellectual and rationalistic. And not only did they feel the allurement of the individual search for truth, the irresistible attraction of the ideas originated in their own brain and not received from outside; but both were tempted farther still from all orthodox pales by their ardent quest for beauty.

"God has inspired me with a vehement love of the beautiful"[1] writes Milton to Deodati. And Blake teaches that "the Poetic Genius is the true man" and the source of all Religions.[2]

Therefore we find in both the high pride of intellectual aims; they are both persuaded that they have an important part to play among men. They both aspire to the highest achievements of literature; and, chiefly in their maturity and old age, both go beyond literature: art becomes for them an instrument of religion. The intellectual ambition that has grown in them since their childhood passes into a desire for religious action. Both become prophets of the Spirit that they feel in themselves.

[1] Bohn, vol. III, p. 494.
[2] Tract: *All religions are one.*

Here culminate in both all pride, all ambition, all aims of life.

Milton, after the failure of the kingdom of the Saints on this earth undertakes to

Justify the ways of God to Man;

And Blake gave his friends the impression: "That the redemption of mankind hangs on the universal diffusion of the doctrines broached in this MS.," namely the manuscript of *Jerusalem*.[1]

Thus three great fundamental traits of character among other minor ones, will bring about a close relationship in the work of Milton and of Blake: their generous pride, their passionate temperament, their ardour for religion and art considered as one.

But the great difference between them has its deep roots also in their characters. Both were proud, but their pride took a different course. Milton's high idea of himself led him to keep a firm control over his nature; he ruled over his own life like an imperious lord. He planned and mapped out his courses of action, and directed his passions into the channels prepared by his intelligence. He put down the flesh mercilessly and boasted of his control over it.[2]

[1] Sampson, *Introduction*, p. 45.
[2] *Doctrine and Discipline of Divorce.*

In similar circumstances, Blake let his strong nature carry him away, and twice fell ill over the disappointment of passion.[1]

Blake's pride took the form of self-assertion and not of self-control. He refused to be bound, and he refused to bind himself. He proclaimed the sanctity of his desire, and would never be gainsaid.

This was with him the pure impatience of all control, for he could otherwise be sensible and shrewd in human affairs: he saw Paine's danger before anybody else, and the politician was saved by taking the visionary's advice.[2]

The difference between the two poets is most marked in the course of their friendships. Milton was as superior to his friends as Blake to his, and fully as self-conscious. But Milton made the best, and Blake the worst of all each came into touch with; because Milton reined in his pride, and was affable, kind and self-controlled: thus he learnt much from inferior men, from Hartlib, and Oldenburg, and Ellwood. And his friends admired him and stood by him to the end. In the bitter times of the Restoration, it is probable that they saved him from persecution, and perhaps he owed them his

---

[1] Ellis, p. 38 and 90–91.
[2] Ellis, p. 162–163, Mona Wilson, p. 50 (Gilchrist).

life.[1] He kept on good terms with people from all parties: Oldenburg and his patrons, the Boyles, were royalists at heart and yet staunch friends of his. It can be said of him that he never lost a friend, and acquired more and more as he grew in years.

Blake, on the contrary, never could keep a friend, or treat one as an equal. He gathered round him at the end of his life a group of young men who considered him with mixed love and wonder, Samuel Palmer, the Linnells, Tatham, and others: but they were the young levites round the old prophet: they listened and said nought, or else asked questions only. All the old friends, one after another, drop out of his life, offended by his uncontrollable temper. Mr. and Mrs. Mathews, who published his first book, and were held up to ridicule in *The Island in the Moon*[2]; the good-natured Hayley who gave him help and employment, and was accused of the worst crimes—in a mystical sense;—Flaxman and Fuseli; and Butts, who kept it up longest and yet in the end became estranged,[3] probably when he saw that his financial help was no longer needed. All, at one time or other, are subject to the bitterest attacks. Blake was

[1] Masson, vol. VI.
[2] Ellis, chap. VII, to IX.
[3] Ellis, p. 406.

one of the best befriended of artists or men of letters: kind friend after kind friend took him in hand only to drop him with awe and wonder after a time. And yet Blake was a kind and loving man: but his temper was uncontrollable and he never wanted to control it.

All that was according to principle: whereas Milton deliberately followed Reason, Blake followed Desire, or the passing mood of the moment; Much of his failure in life is due to that.

The same intolerance accompanied Blake in the intellectual world. There is, of course, an enormous difference between him and Milton in point of culture. Partly, no doubt, Milton's opportunities and splendid education account for the difference, but it is due even more to the difference in receptivity. Milton knew and assimilated everything in the world of letters. Blake, who gathered for himself and by himself immense treasures of culture, had a veritable genius for rejection. He treated his intellectual friends like his living ones. His pugnacity is formidable and indiscriminately manifested. Homer and Ovid, Plato and Cicero,[1] Bacon, Newton, Rousseau, Voltaire, even Swedenborg and Milton, even Isaiah and Ezekiel[2]—not to

[1] *Milton, Preface.*
[2] *Marriage of Heaven and Hell.*

mention Rembrandt and Sir Joshua Reynolds—
are subjected to most violent and often totally incomprehensible attacks.

Both Milton and Blake have the same contempt
for authorities, but while Milton is a true scholar,
Blake carries his total disregard of any achieve-
ment of his predecessors to an absolute indifference
to science and scholarship. He will quietly lay
down the most hair-raising assumptions, and Dr.
Garnett incurs the wrath of Blake's most devoted
and most suggestive English critic by picking up
a few of them[1]:

"That the Greek marbles are copies of the works
of Asiatic patriarchs, that no one painted in oil
except by accident before Vandyke, that ancient
British heroes dwell to this day on Snowdon in
'naked simplicity,' a species of Welsh Mahatmas,
as it would appear."

We can sympathize with Mr. Ellis's anger at the
accusation of madness hurled at Blake, but also
with Dr. Garnett's amazement at the intellectual
self-indulgence of the poet. For it seems that Blake
wrote or said anything that came into his head,
regardless of its objective truth, knowing full well
apparently that he was talking nonsense, often
doing it on purpose to puzzle his audience, suggests

[1] Ellis, p. 173 after quoting Dr. Garnett.

Gilchrist. Then Blake always had a mystical meaning which would explain anything. Surely a predominant element in all his extravagances is simply a wilful lack of intellectual self-control and abandonment to fancy. There is much of the spoilt child in Blake, and perhaps that ordinary human element would go far to explain his apparent "madness."

Thus the element of wilfulness in Blake separates the two poets; and by adding it to the great fundamental resemblances we shall account for most of the variations of the Blakean music upon Miltonic themes.

CHAPTER II

BLAKE was a patient student of Milton. It seems probable that Milton's works were among the few books persistently read by him, Swedenborg's and the Bible being the other great influences. But Milton must have had besides, for Blake, the attraction of a high example to follow. For Milton was not only a religious thinker, but a great poet: he had achieved—the only one to do so—something similar to what Blake wanted to achieve: he had created a great religious epic. So it is easy to understand why, in Crabb Robinson's reminiscences, Milton's name is perhaps the most frequently mentioned.

From his fervid meditations on Milton, as we shall see in examining the creed of the two poets, Blake drew many things that were not in Milton. But he had a real genius of intuition, and he often reveals to us true tendencies of Milton's mind—although he exaggerates the points of contact or of contrast between himself and his predecessor.

To see in what way his mind worked on Milton's ideas, it is important to study first a little of the direct relationship, by imitation or suggestion, between the two bodies of poems. It is unnecessary to hunt out all the similar passages, but some proof must be given, to show how deeply Blake had fed on Milton, and so assimilated Milton's poetry as no longer to distinguish at times between it and his own.   1319997

The direct influence is most evident in *Vala* and in *Milton*. *Vala* is more or less a regular epic, with a tale to tell, and we are able to follow, even though it be from afar, the march of the events. On the contrary, *Jerusalem* is most obscure to the uninitiated, and the influence of Milton, which is ever for clearness and light, is less seen in that poem. But again in *Milton*, necessarily because of the name and subject of this poem, the presence of his conception of his great compeer is more evident in Blake's mind.

Precise comparisons will enable us to see how Blake used and transformed Miltonic Material; and, having seen Blake's mind at work on concrete artistic facts, images and verses, we shall be better able to understand the way in which he treated Milton's more general ideas.

The similarity between Blake's *Urizen* and

Milton's *Satan* has often been pointed out.[1] The resemblance is one of position chiefly, not of character. Urizen attempts to seize the Supreme Power; he falls; he establishes his dominion on Earth over all men by means of false religions; he is finally conquered by Jesus. The main lines of his adventure are thus comparable to Satan's in Milton. But the precise episodes and the meanings given to them are far indeed from Milton's world of ideas or art. Still in many cases we can see in Blake's work a transposition of Milton's into another world.

In the first canto of *Vala*, Urizen's conspiracy with Lubah recalls Satan's with Beelzebub:[2]

Soon as midnight brought on the dusky hour,
Friendliest to sleep and silence, he resolv'd
With all his legions to dislodge, and leave
Unworship'd, unobey'd, the throne supreme,
Contemptuous; and his next subordinate
Awaking, thus to him in secret spake.

"Sleep'st thou, companion dear! what sleep can
　　　close
Thy eyelids, and remember'st what decree
Of yesterday, so late hath pass'd the lips

[1] Cf. P. Berger's *Blake*.
[2] Book V, 666.

Of heav'n's Almighty? Thou to me thy thoughts
Wast wont, I mine to thee was wont t'impart:
Both waking we were one; how then can now
Thy sleep dissent? Assemble thou
Of all those myriads which we lead the chief:
Tell them, that by command, ere yet dim night
Her shadowy cloud withdraws, I am to haste
(And all who under me their banners wave)
Homeward, with flying march, where we possess
The quarters of the north."

Thus Satan. And, while Albion's family

Slept round on hills and valleys in the reign of his
  love,
Urizen awoke and Luvah awoke, and they conferred,
  thus[1]:

"Thou Luvah," said the Prince of Light, "behold our
  our sons and daughters,
"Repose on beds. Let them sleep on; do thou alone
  depart
"Into thy wished kingdom, where, in Majesty and
  power,
"We may create a throne. Deep in the North I place
  my lot,
"Thou in the South. Listen attentive. In silence of this
  night,

[1] *Vala*, I, 445.

"I will infold the universal tent in clouds opaque, while
    thou
"Seizest the chariots of the morning——"

Urizen with darkness overspreading all the armies
Sent round his heralds secretly commanding to depart
Into the North. Sudden with thunder's sound his
    multitudes
Retreat from the fierce light, all sons of Urizen at once,
Mustering together in thick clouds.

We have here a development of the Miltonic
scene: more precise directions, more complex
movements, a different meaning, but the same
general lines.

And the same fall into the abyss overtakes the
adventurers, at once in Blake:

Sudden, down they fell all together into an unknown
    space,
Deep, horrible, without end, from Beulah separate,
    far beneath—,

but in Milton only as the grand termination of the
battle in Heaven.

The journeys of Urizen in the sixth Night of
Vala, his explorations through the dark world of
Urthona are strongly reminiscent of Satan's travels
through outer Hell and Chaos.

As Satan meets his family at the gates of Hell,
Urizen comes unawares upon his three daughters:

Lo, three terrific women at the verge of the bright
    flood
Who would not suffer him to approach, but drove
    him back with storm
Urizen knew them not and thus addressed the spirits
    of darkness:
"Who art thou, eldest woman, sitting wrapped up in
    these thy clouds?"

.   .   .   .

Then Urizen raised his spear, but they reared up a wall
    of rock,
They gave a scream,—they knew their father: Urizen
    knew his daughters
He knew they were his children, ruined in his ruined
    world.[1]

Transposed into a weirder atmosphere, sur-
charged with mystic meaning, we find all the chief
traits of the Miltonic episode; the meeting, the
father not knowing his children, the repulse of the
wanderer by his progeny, the preparations for a
fight, and the final recognition.

There is more terror and power in Milton, but
there is in Blake a subtler atmosphere of mystical

[1] *Vala*, VI, 5.

dread, a more disturbing touch of the supernatural.

And withal there is no direct imitation, only a
parallelism of poetic invention which probably
was hardly conscious in Blake's mind. The rendering, the style, the meaning, are different, though
the architecture of the passage is the same.

> Before the gates there sat[1]
> On either side a formidable shape—
>   —black it stood as night,
> Fierce as ten Furies, terrible as hell,
> And shook a dreadful dart; what seemed his head
> The likeness of a kingly crown had on—

And Satan addresses him thus:

> "Whence and what art thou, execrable shape,
> That dar'st, though grim and terrible, advance
> Thy miscreated front athwart my way
> To yonder gates?"

And the spears are lifted:

> Each at the head
> Levelled his deadly aim.

Then come the explanations; but all the end part

---

[1] *Paradise Lost*, II, 648.

is condensed in Blake's rendering into the brief statement:

They gave a scream, they knew their father: Urizen knew his daughters.

Blake has no patience: just as he settled in two lines the Fall of Urizen and his sons, not caring to imitate at that point the Miltonic description of wars in Heaven, here he curtails all details of the meeting between father and progeny. He seems to want to get rid quickly of the load of imitation he has assumed, and bungles out of both episodes.

Then the whole of Night VI, is hardly more than a splendid paraphrase of Milton's description of the voyage through Chaos:

> Nigh foundered on he fares,
> Treading the crude consistence, half on foot
> Half flying—
> O'er bog or steep, through strait, rough, dense, or
>   rare,
> With head, hands, wings or feet, pursues his way,
> And swims, or sinks, or wades, or creeps, or flies.[1]

Thus Satan. And thus Urizen[2]:

[1] *Paradise Lost*, II. 940.
[2] Night VI, 72.

Urizen replied not, on his way
He took high-sounding over hills and desert, floods and
    chasms
Infinite was his labour, without end his travel. He
    strove
In vain, for hideous monsters of the deep annoyed him
    sore,
Scaled and finned with iron and brass, devoured the
    path before him,
Incessant with the conflict. On he bent his weary
    steps
Making a path towards the dark world of Urthona.
When he had passed the Southern terrors he
    approached the East,
Void, pathless, beaten with eternal sleet, and eternal
    rain and hail.
No form was there, no living thing, and yet his way
    lay through
This dismal world. He stood a while and looked back
    over his
Terrific voyages—hills and dales of torment and
    despair
Sighing and weeping a fresh tear.[1]

This can compare with Milton's best:

Before their eyes in sudden view appear
The secrets of the hoary deep, a dark
Illimitable ocean, without bound,

[1] VI, 137.

Without dimension, where length, breadth and
    highth,
And time and place are lost; where eldest Night
And Chaos, ancestors of Nature, hold
Eternal anarchy amidst the noise
Of endless wars, and by confusion stand.[1]

But nothing in Blake approaches the tremendous
interview of the Archangel and Chaos.[2]

T'whom Satan turning boldly, thus: "Ye Powers,
And Spirits of this nethermost abyss,
Chaos and ancient night, I come no spy
With purpose to explore or to disturb
The secrets of your realm."

In precision of description and in sheer power,
Milton excels, because of his clear hard imagination; in suggestion of imprecise and haunting
dangers, of mystical incomprehensible terror, Blake
is supreme. Thus he describes the state of the
fallen children of Urizen, more impressively,
because more obscurely, than even Milton pictures
his "confounded" rebels:

They wander, moping, in their heart a sun and weary
    moon,

[1] *Paradise Lost*, II, 890.
[2] *Paradise Lost*, II, 967.

An universe of fiery constellations in their brain,
An earth of wintry woe beneath their feet, and round
    their loins
Waters, or winds of clouds, lightnings and pestilential
    plagues;
Beyond the bounds of their own self their senses cannot
    reach.
As the tree knoweth not what is outside its leaves and
    bark,
And yet it drinks the Summer joy and fears the
    Winter sorrow,
So in the region of the grave none knows his dark
    compeer,
Though he partakes of his dire woes.[1]

In Milton, reason predominates, a logical hard
vision of things; but Blake lets himself go to the
violence and the incomprehensible longings of his
desire, and his imagination is ever striving after

Thoughts beyond the reaches of our souls.

There is no terror for Milton in the unknown
world: because that world is not to him unknown;
and because his feelings are well daunted by his
powerful will, and he confronts dread with a
masterful pride of Intellect; he can face either Satan
raging or God in his glory and not fear, so com-

VI, 90.

pletely is he the emperor of his soul. But Blake has abdicated reason and self-control: he follows his Imagination into the unknowable abyss. When his Pride is roused, he also can face and overcome Terror, but he feels it ever deeply. He has upon him the dread of the unknowable ; and he neither could nor would explain his myths clearly and reasonably, because the object of his search lay beyond the clear and the reasonable.

This temper is in all his prophetic writings. And so perhaps it is a mistake, and a sin against the Spirit of Blake, to try and understand logically all his mythology. He takes us into a grand, obscure and terrifying world, a world which is beyond Light; and if the gloom is dispelled and the light breaks in, the illusion vanishes and the art is dead. In the grandest effects of the *Prophetic Books*, the incomprehensible is perhaps an element not to be eliminated.

Thus the comparison between the art of the two poets reveals to us that the Miltonic is only one element in Blake, the reasonable element, it might be named; and it is overlaid with many strange seas in which there are jewels also.

Another Miltonic theme handled by Blake is the plucking of the apple. The gestures of the Persons are similar, but how different, even in their similarity, are the words and the implications.

Thus Enitharmon offers the fruit to Los[1]:

"When in the deeps beneath I gathered of this ruddy
     fruit,
It was by that I knew that I had sinned, and I knew
That, without ransom, I could not be saved from
     Eternal Death,
That life lives upon death, and by devouring appetite
All things subsist on one another. Thenceforth in
     despair
I spend my glowing times; but thou art strong and
     mighty thou
To bear this self-contrition. Take then, eat thou also of
The fruit and give me proof of life eternal or I die."

Then Los pluck'd the fruit, and ate and sat down in
     despair
And must have surely given himself to death eternal
     but
Urthona's spectre ministering within him comforted
As medium between him and Enitharmon, but this
     union
Was not to be effected without cares and sorrows and
     troubles,
Six thousand years of self-denial and bitter contrition.

We find here as in Milton, the weaker woman

[1] *Night* VII, 381.

leaning upon the man, even to bear her guilt, the despair of the man, the bitter contention between the guilty pair, the final reconciliation, and the ultimate salvation after destiny has run its course. But all these elements are scarcely recognizable in Blake's handling; and each word means something different from our meaning and Milton's.

Blake has even more closely imitated, although in the same fantastic manner, the final punishment which visits Satan in his triumph, when[1]

> His visage drawn he felt to sharp and spare,
> His arms clung to his ribs, his legs entwining
> Each other, till supplanted down he fell,
> A monstrous serpent on his belly prone,
> Reluctant—

In the Night VIII of *Vala*, Urizen[2]

> sat stonied upon his rock
> Forgetful of his own laws, petrifying he began to
>   embrace
> The shadowy female. Since life cannot be quenched,
>   life exuded,
> His eyes shot forward, then his breathing nostrils
>   drawn forth,
> Scales covered over a cold forehead and a neck out-
>   stretched

[1] *Paradise Lost*, X, 511.
[2] 413.

Into the deep to seize the shadow. Scales his neck and
    bosom
Covered; scales his hands and feet. Upon his belly[1]
    falling
Outstretched through the immense, his mouth wide
    open, tongueless,
His teeth a triple row, he strove to seize the shadow in
    vain
And his immense tail lashed the abyss.

In the poem entitled *Milton* there is less imitation
of the elder poet, but perhaps more influence, and
the Miltonic elements and thoughts are farther
and farther from Milton. We have here the
extreme instance of Blake's power of transforming
beyond bourne or reason what he derived from a
saner mind.

The whole theme has little to do with the real
Milton. Yet in Blake's mind, the subject of the
poem was probably the tale of a new reincarnation
of Milton, the real man:

Milton of the Land of Albion should up ascend
Forwards from Ulro from the Vale of Felpham and
    set free
Orc from his chain of Jealousy.[2]

---

[1] The word points to a precise reminiscence.
[2] *Milton*, p. 18.

Milton's work was for Blake "prophecy," religious poetry or something equally liberating and essential in the seer's system. Thus we can take the very fact that the poem is called *Milton* as a sign of a deep influence consciously received by Blake.

But beyond that, Blake gives us proof that he means to sing of the real poet Milton: thus he refers to his private life.[1]

Then Milton knew that the three heavens of Beulah
     were beheld
By him on earth in his bright pilgrimage of sixty
     years
In the three females whom his wives and these three
     whom his daughters.

And it is a grand piece of poetical intuition on Blake's part, to set Milton to fight Urizen, since

Los and Enitharmon knew that Satan is Urizen.[2]

and since in *Paradise Lost* the real Adversary and and Pursuer of Satan is the poet himself. The fantastical fight is thus described by Blake: from the river Jordan, Urizen poured on

[1] *Milton*, p. 14 and 16.
[2] Supplementary pages, p. 8, Ellis and Yeats' edition.

To Milton's brain the icy fluid from his broad cold
     palm.
But Milton took of the red clay of Succoth, moulding it
     with care
Between his palms and filling up the furrows of many
     years,
Beginning at the feet of Urizen and on the bones
Creating new flesh on the Demon cold and building
     him.
          Silent Milton stood before
The darkened Urizen, as the sculptor silent stands
     before
His forming image; he walks round it patient labour-
     ing.[1]

No doubt it is also under Milton's influence that
Satan becomes the chief hero of the prophecy,
instead of Urizen, or rather as a new form of
Urizen.

Blake also makes Satan the Father of Sin and
Death[2]; and the Miltonic allegory must have
worked strongly on Blake's imagination, since
we find him, unconsciously perhaps, quoting the
very words of Milton, in a speech of Leutha[3]:

          I weeping hid in Satan's inmost brain
But when the Gnomes refused to labour more, with
     blandishment

[1] P. 17 and 18.   [2] P. 28.   [3] P. 9.

I came forth from the head of Satan; back the Gnomes
   recoiled
And called me Sin and for a sign portentous held me.

Thus Milton had sung of the rebel host's affright,
in Sin's words to Satan:

> Out of thy head I sprung[3]; amazement seized
> All the host of heaven; back they recoiled afraid
> At first, and called me Sin, and for a sign
> Portentous held me.[1]

A last characteristic instance of Blake's way of
widening the paths broken by Milton is in the
address to the reader, on rhythm, at the beginning
of *Jerusalem*. Blake is imitating the noble prose
prefaced to *Paradise Lost*, and to put it vulgarly,
"trying to go one better."

Milton prided himself for having set an example.

"The first in English of ancient liberty recovered
to Heroic Poem from the troublesome and modern
bondage of Riming."

And, thereupon, Blake:

"When this Verse was first dictated to me, I
consider'd a monotonous cadence like that used by
Milton and Shakespeare, and all writers of English
Blank Verse, derived from the modern bondage of

[1] *Paradise Lost*, II, 758.

Riming, to be a necessary and indispensable part of Verse. But I soon found that in the mouth of a true Orator such monotony was not only awkward, but as much a bondage as rime itself."

And Blake proceeds mercilessly to apply Milton's own principle of liberty to much that Milton had respected.

We shall find this attitude of reckless and rebellious discipleship to be a frequent one in our study of Blake's relationship to Milton.

It would be interesting to compare the art of the two poets; and although we are concerned here chiefly with their philosophy, a mention of a few of the larger characteristics may be germane to our purpose.

The world of Milton's poems is that of Blake's: whether it be the infernal world proper, or the wider Cosmos in which the whole Solar system is

> as a star
> Of smallest magnitude close by the moon.[1]

Blake moves at ease in the infinite spaces; he is perhaps more at home in them than Milton: he takes them more easily as granted. But that is only because he has been, so to speak, brought up in it, by Milton himself. The first poet had to

[1] *Paradise Lost*, II, 1,051.

create that world of immensity, his follower had only to come into it.

Therefore Blake is much more careless than Milton: Milton is conscious that he has raised a delicate, if grand, structure: he is afraid of possible havoc, when

> The starry cope
> Of heaven perhaps, or all the elements
> At least had gone to wrack, disturbed and torn.[1]

And this havoc is certainly wrought by Blake, who careers recklessly through shattered solar systems.

Blake comes into the harmonious world of Milton—and he would have appreciated this as a compliment—much like Satan into the world of this earth: he seems composed at times, but that sharp-sighted angel,

> The same whom John saw also in the sun,

would have said of Blake, as of the Rebel Archangel:[2]

> I descried his way,
> Bent all on speed, and marked his aery gait
> But on the mount that lies from Eden north
> Where he first lighted, soon discerned his looks
> Alien from heaven, with passions foul obscured.

[1] *Paradise Lost*, IV, 992.   [2] *Paradise Lost*, IV, 566.

And Uriel might well add:

Mine eye pursued him still, but under shade
Lost sight of him.

For often indeed do we lose sight of Blake's
course through his astronomical world; and it
would be no mean task to map out the Blakean
Cosmos, whereas Milton's is clear and simple to
the mind's eye.

Both are absolute masters of the shorter lyrical
forms, but in his technique in the longer poems,
Blake has not the direct, simple and majestic
melody of Milton, as in:

So were I equalled with them in renown,

Or:

Hurled headlong flaming from the ethereal sky
With hideous ruin and combustion, down
To bottomless perdition.

Blake has a more supple and less strong rhythm:

What shall we do for thee, o lovely mild Jerusalem.[1]

But the terrible is as easily within his power:

[1] *Jerusalem*, p. 12.

I will break thee into shivers, and melt thee in the
    furnaces of death
I will cast thee into forms of abhorrence and torment
    if thou
Desist not from thine own will and obey not my stern
    command.[1]

And the length of the lines often adds to their power. In their art as in their thought, the relationship is the same: Milton controls and concentrates, Blake lets go and expands. Milton is reason and Blake is desire. And thus Blake reaches at times a sort of feline rhythm, leaping on velvet paws, quite beyond Milton's simpler art:

Watching his time with glowing eyes to leap upon his
    prey.[2]

[1] *Jerusalem*, p. 8.
[2] *Jerusalem*, p. 8.

CHAPTER III

I. PRINCIPLES

THE chief points of relationship between Blake and Milton, both in similarity and in difference spring from their views of morality.

Both had been brought up in an intensely religious atmosphere; for both, morality was the fundamental thing in life; this is shown by the large place occupied by the theories of the Fall in their systems of thought. For both, the influence of their ethics on their metaphysics is predominant; and their metaphysics are little more than an abstract scheme of justification of their moral views. It is therefore necessary, before comparing their ideas of the Fall, and then their metaphysics, to set side by side their principles of morality.

Blake explains his position in antagonism to Milton's in *The Marriage of Heaven and Hell:*

"Those who restrain Desire do so because theirs is weak enough to be restrained; and the restrainer or Reason usurps its place and governs the unwilling.

"And, being restrained, it by degrees becomes passive till it is only the shadow of Desire.

"The history of this is written in *Paradise Lost* and the Governor, or Reason, is called Messiah.

"And the original Archangel, or possessor of the command of the Heavenly Host, is call'd the Devil or Satan, and his children are called Sin and Death.

"But in the Book of Job, Milton's Messiah is called Satan.

"For this history has been adopted by both parties.

"It indeed appeared to Reason as if Desire was cast out; but the Devil's account is that the Messiah fell, and formed a Heaven of what he stole from the Abyss.[1]

"This is shown in the Gospel, where he prays to the Father to send the Comforter, or Desire, that Reason may have Ideas to build on; the Jehovah of the Bible being no other than he who dwells in flaming fire.

"Know that after Christ's death, he became Jehovah.

"But in Milton, the Father is Destiny, the Son

---

[1] This is Blake's account of the myth he develops in the Prophecies, where "Messiah," i.e., Reason, is Urizen.

a Ratio of the five senses and the Holy Ghost Vacuum.

"Note.—The reason Milton wrote in fetters when he wrote of angels and God, and at liberty when of Devils and Hell, is because he was a true poet and of the Devil's party without knowing it."

We can discern clearly the similarities between the two poets' ideas.

Both hold the same view of the dual nature of man: Desire and Reason.

Milton explains himself as precisely as Blake, when he makes Michael say to Adam[1]:

> Since thy original lapse, true liberty
> Is lost (which always with right reason dwells
> Twinn'd, and from her hath no dividual being).
> Reason in man obscur'd, or not obey'd,
> Immediately inordinate desires,
> And upstart passions, catch the government
> From Reason; and to servitude reduce
> Man, till then free.

Both poets more or less explicitly admit the necessity of the two parts of man; both admit their antagonism; both want to establish harmony between them.

[1] *Paradise Lost*, XII, 82.

Here they part. Blake wants Desire to be free from the control of Reason. Reason follows Desire, is enlarged and transfigured in the process, and transformed into what Blake calls Imagination, or the Poetic Genius:

"As the true method of Knowledge is Experiment, the true faculty of knowing must be the faculty which experiences."[1]

This sounds like an ultra-rational view of "Reason," but Blake adds:

"This Faculty I treat of: that the Poetic Genius is the true man." Reason is thus not so much cast out by Blake as transformed into a servant of Desire.

But for Milton the harmony is reversed, and Reason must lead Desire: otherwise it is the Fall[2]:

> For understanding rul'd not; and the will
> Heard not her lore, both in subjection now
> To sensual appetite, who from beneath
> Usurping, over sov'reign reason claim'd
> Superior sway.

The two poets have the same view of the moral world, but they do not give priority to the same element.

[1] *All Religions are one.*
[2] *Paradise Lost*, IX, 1128.

This difference overlays all resemblances, and is the source of many differences. It is in relation with the nature of each poet's temperament: Blake's, exuberant, overflowing with sympathy for all life and desire; Milton's, concentrated, centred on self-respect and self-restraint, with fierce rejection of vice and vulgarity.

II. GENERAL SIMILARITIES

And yet this fundamental difference is greater in theory than in fact.

As Blake points out, Milton was "a true Poet, and of the Devil's party without knowing it." To put it less mythologically, Milton was full of passions of all kinds, and therefore in the very depth of his nature there was a sympathy for passion. Hence the favourable artistic presentation of Satan, contrasting with the bitter intellectual denunciation of him.

The Miltonic world of thought rests on the antagonism between Desire and Reason, on the very existence of Satan; it would cease to exist if Satan disappeared. And there is no doubt that Milton thought his world good, and would not gladly have spared his Satan.

Blake, as is usual with him, voices freely feelings

which were but semi-conscious in Milton, and
boldly theorizes:

"Without contraries is no progression. Attraction and Repulsion, Reason and Energy, Love
and Hate, are necessary to Human existence."

And again:

"One portion of being is the Prolific, the other
the Devouring—the Prolific would cease to be
Prolific unless the Devourer, as a sea, received the
excess of his delights—these two classes of men
are always upon earth and they should be enemies:
whoever tries to reconcile them seeks to destroy
existence."[1]

These reflections might well come to Blake from
his meditations on *Paradise Lost*. Not that this is
how Blake came by them, but they might spring
from the Miltonic passage where God says he will
create this world to repair the loss of the Fallen
Angels:

> But lest his heart[2] exalt him, in the harm
> Already done, to have dispeopled heav'n,
> (My damage fondly deem'd!) I can repair
> That detriment, if such it be, to lose
> Self-lost; and in a moment will create
> Another world; out of one man, a race

---

[1] *The Marriage of Heaven and Hell.*
[2] Satan's *Paradise Lost*, VII, 150.

Of men innumerable there to dwell,
Not here; till by degrees of merit rais'd,
They open to themselves at length the way
Up hither; under long obedience try'd:
And earth be chang'd to heav'n, and heav'n to
    earth,
One kingdom, joy, and union without end.
Meanwhile inhabit lax, ye Pow'rs of heav'n!

To put it in Blake's more fanciful language, the Prolific would not have been Prolific, had not the Devourer, as a sea, received His excess.

Thus what is to Milton an artistic, or sentimental, necessity, becomes for Blake an intellectual one. Again and again we come upon this peculiar relationship of the two: Blake expressing, by forcing them into what would have been paradox to Milton's mind, some of Milton's feelings.

But Milton also recognized that Good and Evil, Reason and Desire, "are necessary to human existence "[1]:

"Good and Evil we know in the field of this world grow up together almost inseparably; and the knowledge of good is so involved and inter-woven with the knowledge of evil, and in so many cunning resemblances hardly to be discerned, that those confused seeds which were imposed upon

[1] *Areopagitica*, Bohn, p. 67.

Psyche as an incessant labour to cull out, and sort asunder, were not more intermixed. It was from out the rind of one apple tasted, that the knowledge of good and evil, as two twins cleaving together, leaped forth into the world. And perhaps this is that doom which Adam fell into of knowing good and evil; that is to say, of knowing good by evil.

"As therefore the state of man now is; what wisdom can there be to choose, what continence to forbear, without the knowledge of evil? He that can apprehend and consider vice with all her baits and seeming pleasures, and yet abstain, and yet distinguish, and yet prefer that which is truly better, he is the true warfaring Christian. I cannot praise a fugitive and cloistered virtue, unexercised and unbreathed, that never sallies out and seeks her adversary, but slinks out of the race."

Thus Milton's sympathies with the "Devil's party, without knowing it" go some way towards bridging the differences between the two poets.

But there is more perhaps in the fact that Milton is the great vindicator of desire: with restrictions, and within certain bounds, though on the whole of the great, sound, normal desires of human nature.

Milton proclaims the holiness of the body because the body is made of matter, and matter is a part of God: He says of the origin of matter:

"There remains but one solution of the difficulty —namely that all things are of God."[1]

And therefore:

"The original matter of which we speak is not to be looked upon as an evil or trivial thing, but as intrinsically good, and the chief productive stock of every subsequent good."[2]

Therefore the desires inherent in matter are good, and the normal man fulfils God's ends when satisfying his own desires:

> Our maker bids increase, who bids abstain,
> But our destroyer, foe to God and Man.

Hence that hymn to wedded love, which is a hymn to sensual love, in the description of Life in Paradise, the normal holy life of man:

> Far be it, that I should write thee sin or blame,
> Or think thee unbefitting holiest place
> Perpetual fountain of domestic sweets.[3]

And we read in the *Tetrachordon*[4]:

[1] *Treatise of Christian Doctrine*, Bohn, p. 178.
[2] Ditto, p. 179.
[3] *Paradise Lost*, IV, 745-775.
[4] P. 331.

"Whereof lest we should be too timorous, in the awe that our flat sages would form us and dress us, wisest Solomon among his gravest proverbs countenances a kind of ravishment and erring fondness in the entertainment of wedded leisures, and in the Song of Songs, which is generally believed, even in the jolliest expressions, to figure the spousals of the Church with Christ, sings of a thousand raptures between those two lovely ones far on the hither side of carnal enjoyment."

This very important vein in Milton's constitution is one which establishes deep similarity between him and Blake; and makes many differences a mere matter of words.

Then, just as Milton is subject to Desire, so is Blake subject to Reason, and this brings them even more together. Blake, even in spite of himself, and like all human minds, has to rely very largely on Reason. None could argue more logically when the mood was on him than this contemner of Logic.[1] Indeed we shall see when we come to the Metaphysics of the two poets that Blake often soars far above Milton into the thin air of abstract speculation.

And even in his ethics, Blake could not, and did

[1] As M. Berger has pointed out in reference to the pamphlets *On Natural Religion*, etc.

not, get rid of the omnipresent test of Reason. In spite of his glorification of desire generally, he condemns a whole category of desires: those that centre round the self: chiefly egoism, the love of domination, the love of revenge. All through the longer prophecies, he preaches Self-annihilation:

Selfhood must be put off and annihilated alway,
To cleanse the face of my spirit by self-examination.
To Bathe in the waters of Life; to wash off the Not Human,
To come in Self-annihilation and the grandeur of Inspiration.[1]

In this repudiation of Egoism there is first a feeling of love for all that exists, but there is also the sense that Egoism is opposed to the Universal Brotherhood, to the Human imagination, or, to put it more clearly, that Selfhood is a mistake, since we are all members of one another, since

Mutual in one another's love and wrath all renewing
We live as One Man: for, contracting our infinite senses
We behold multitude; or expanding we behold as one.[2]

[1] *Milton*, p. 42-43.
[2] *Jerusalem*, p. 38, 16.

Thus, in fact, Blake and Milton nearly meet for most practical purposes half-way between their opposed theoretical grounds: since Milton does not exclude all Desire, and Blake does exclude some desires, but cannot altogether do away with Reason.

Then there is much similarity in the ideal of each poet: the Imagination of Blake has much in common with the Reason of Milton. Both are essentially the voice of God in each individual man:

Milton holds that Christ came into man for "The illumination of the understanding."

"To infuse from above new and supernatural faculties into the minds of the renovated."[1]

And this Divine Intelligence in us is the Reason we must follow. In a similar spirit Blake writes:

"He who despises and mocks a Mental Gift in another—mocks Jesus the Giver of every mental gift."[2]

III. MORALITY AS LIBERTY

From this similar conception of the ruling principle in every man both poets derive the same conception of moral and intellectual liberty: let the Normal Individual create his own rules:

[1] *Treatise of Christian Doctrine*, p. 299 and 328.
[2] *Jerusalem*, p. 77.

"I know of no other Christianity and of no other
Gospel than the liberty both of body and mind to
exercise the Divine arts of Imagination,"[1] says
Blake, and Milton might have said it, since he
writes:

"Christian liberty is that whereby we are loosed
as it were by enfranchisement, through Christ our
deliverer, from the bondage of sin, and consequently from the rule of the law and of man—
that we may serve God in love through the
guidance of the Spirit of Truth."[2]

For both poets Morality is Liberty: once the
inner man is regenerated, his right, nay, his duty
is to do what he wants to do, for, as Milton
expresses it:

"The mind of Christ is in him."[3]

and

"The rule of judgment will be the conscience
of each individual"[4]

Blake only extended to its fullest this principle
of Milton when he said to Crabb Robinson:
"That was the fault of Plato: he knew of nothing

[1] *Jerusalem*, p. 77.
[2] *Treatise of Christian Doctrine*, p. 389-399.
[3] *T. C. D.*, p. 444.
[4] *T. C. D.*, p. 483.

but the Virtues and Vices. There is nothing in all that. Everything is good in God's eyes."[1]

What Blake condemns chiefly under the name of Reason, is in reality Law; and this brings him very near Milton.

Urizen, the great Accursed one of *The Prophetic Books*, is the Father of all Law:

> So, I unfold my darkness, and on
> This rock place, with strong hand, the Book
> Of Eternal Brass, written in my solitude:
> One Command, one joy, one desire,
> One curse, one weight, one measure,
> One King, one God, one Law.[2]

The Fall is largely for Blake the setting up of Law; and the Regeneration the gradual deliverance of man from this "Web of Urizen."

Milton is less mythological and much more explicit on this point; he gives us a light to understand Blake by, when he explains in sober prose that the origin of all Law is in the Fall:

"No man who knows aught can be so stupid to deny that all men were naturally born free—and they had lived so, till from the root of Adam's transgression falling among themselves to do

---

[1] Crabb Robinson's Diary, Symons, p. 288.
[2] *The Book of Urizen*, ch. II.

wrong and violence—they agreed by common league to bind each other.—Hence came cities, towns and commonwealths."[1]

Both poets see in the Fall the origin of Law; Milton, besides, sees the necessity of Law for the fallen ones; but both are again at one in proclaiming that for the regenerate all Law is abolished.

Milton sets down that:

"Paul expressly asserts that the law is not made for the righteous man."[2] Christ came to free us from all rule:

"The entire Mosaic law was abolished. We are absolved from subjection to the decalogue as fully as to the rest of the law."[3]

Blake picturesquely applies the same idea to the conduct cf Christ:

"Now hear how he has given his Sanction to the law of ten commandments. Did he not mock at the Sabbath, and so mock the Sabbath's God; murder those who were murder'd because of Him; turn away the law from the woman taken in adultery; steal the labour of others to support Him; bear false witness when he omitted making a defence before Pilate; covet when he pray'd for his disciples, and when He bid them shake off the

[1] *Tenure of Kings and Magistrates*, p. 9.
[2] *T. C. D.*, p. 391.
[3] *T. C. D.*, p. 387.

dust of their feet against such as refused to lodge
them? I tell you no virtue can exist without
breaking these ten commandments."[1]

And the whole of *The Everlasting Gospel* runs
on the same theme.

Milton is less piquant, but his application of the
idea of liberty to the practical domain of politics
and life reaches much further than Blake's para-
doxes. The spirit of both is the same.

IV.   RELIGIOUS AND POLITICAL LIBERTY

For both, the great and essential application of
the principle of liberty was in the domain of
religion. Both had the same positive hatred of
priestcraft.

For both the function of the priest is an usurpa-
tion. Milton writes:[2]

"And this all Christians ought to know, that the
title of clergy St. Peter gave to all God's people,
till pope Higinus and the succeeding prelates took
it from them, appropriating that name to themselves and their priests only; and condemning the
rest of God's inheritance to an injurious and
alienate condition of laity, they separated from
them by local partitions in churches, through their

[1] *Marriage of Heaven and Hell:* in fine.
[2] *Reason of Church Government,* p. 493.

gross ignorance and pride imitating the old temple, and excluding the members of Christ from the property of being members, the bearing of orderly and fit offices in the ecclesiastical body; as if they had meant to sew up that Jewish veil, which Christ by his death on the cross rent in sunder. Although these usurpers could not so presently overmaster the liberties and lawful titles of God's freeborn church, but that Origen, being yet a layman, expounded the scriptures publicly."

And Blake sings:

Of the primeval Priest's assum'd power,
When Eternals spurn'd back his Religion
And gave him a place in the North,
Obscure, shadowy, void, solitary.
Eternals! I hear your call gladly,
Dictate swift winged words, and fear not
To unfold your dark visions of torment.[1]

Both enlarge their hatred of priestcraft into a principle of explanation of the world history: the revolutions and the catastrophes of man's societies have chiefly come because of wrong religions, and wrong religions have been established and kept up by the greed of the priests.

[1] *Preludium to the First Book of Urizen.*

Blake mentions

the priest's overgorged abdomen.[1]

with the same fury of condemnation as Milton, in *Lycidas:* the "blind mouths" of orthodox religion.

Blake explains that

"a system was formed, which some took advantage of, and enslav'd the vulgar by attempting to realize or abstract the Mental Deities from their objects; thus began Priesthood."[2]

And Milton stigmatizes the same "race of wicked deceivers" which did away with the "lovely virgin truth" and ursurped power over man.[3]

For both poets, the type and model of religious oppression was the Church of Rome. In his Illustrations to *Europe*, Blake has a repellent picture of papal superstition.[4] In his *Song of Liberty*, he calls out:

"Golden Spain, burst the barriers of old Rome!

Cast thy keys o Rome, into the deep, down falling, even to eternity down falling,

And weep"

---

[1] *Vala*, IX, 249.
[2] *Marriage of Heaven and Hell.*
[3] *Areopagitica*, ed. Garnett, p. 35.
[4] Described by Swinburne in *Blake*, p. 239.

Blake has a general idea that this world, and our religions, worship Satan:

"The Accuser who is the God of this World."[1]
And this worship is particularly led by Roman Catholicism.

Milton, similarly, made at seventeen years old an over-ferocious attack on the Pope in his verses *On the Fifth of November* and in his old age, writing his last pamphlet *On Toleration*, refuses Roman Catholicism alone the liberty allowed every variety of creeds. In the youthful—and somewhat puerile —poem, he describes the alliance between Satan and the Pope; and in his mature poems, he refers to the Catholic Middle Ages as the time

When all our fathers worshipped stocks and stones.[2]

Blake also carried on the patristic tradition, handed down to him by Milton, that old religions had been founded by devils:

They saw Urizen give his laws to the nations
By the hands of the children of Los.
    The human race began to wither.
These were the Churches, Hospitals, Castles,
    Palaces,

[1] *The Gates of Paradise.*
[2] *On the late massacre in Piedmont.* Sonnet.

Like nets and gins and traps, to catch the joys of
   Eternity,
And all the rest a desert,
Till, like a dream, Eternity was obliterated, and
   erased.[1]

But neither Milton nor Blake refrain from apply-
ing the same idea—or a very similar one—to
modern religions. In Blake's Mind, Urizen was
still in Power; Milton describes the rise of the
"race of wicked deceivers" after the coming of
Christ; and in his picture of the course of history
at the end of *Paradise Lost*, he omits to mention
the Reformation; for both poets, Religious Evil
was still upon the Earth, only to cease with the
Last Judgment.

To both also religious Liberty was the chief con-
cern even of politics proper. In Milton's advice
to Cromwell, at the end of the *Second Defence*
the chief anxiety of the poet was that the Protector's
religious policy should be right. And his objections
to Cromwell's government were on religious
grounds.[2]

To ensure religious liberty, or rather liberty of
thought: that was for both poets the aim of government. Neither seems to have cared much for the

[1] *The Song of Los.*
[2] Cf. Masson, vol. IV, p. 615; vol. V, 297–298, etc.

exercise of political rights. Milton entirely approved of the Protector's single-handed reign, and never wished to oppose to it any control by the people; at most, only to add to it the help of a few friends. And Blake lived peacefully and contentedly without seeming to perceive the existence of a government opposed to all his principles. As long as he could "think what he pleased," he was satisfied also.

Samuel Palmer reports of Blake in his old age[1]:

"The Bible, he said, was the book of Liberty, and Christianity the regeneration of nations."

Milton might have spoken those words. For him also Liberty is divinely founded; Adam says of God:

> man over men
> He made not Lord: such title to Himself
> Reserving, human left from human free.[2]

Tyranny over man is a sacrilege:

"If we should consider attentively the countenance of a man, and inquire after whose image so noble a creature were framed, would not any one that heard him presently make answer, that he was made after the image of God himself?

---

[1] Ellis, *The Real Blake*, p. 427.
[2] *Paradise Lost*, XII, 70.

Being therefore peculiarly God's own, and consequently things that are to be given to him, we are entirely free by nature, and cannot without the greatest sacrilege imaginable be reduced into a condition of slavery to any man, especially to a wicked, unjust, cruel tyrant."[1]

For both poets also man's liberty is essentially in himself, the outside forms of government are of little importance : they are modelled upon the moral state of the citizens.

A note of Blake's runs thus[2] :

"If men were wise, Princes, the most arbitrary, could not hurt them. If they are not wise, the freest government is compelled to be a tyranny."

This is the fundamental principle of Milton's politics: the only guarantee of political liberty is the inner liberty of man's soul: wisdom, reason. Blake is here at a disadvantage: he has no such precise conception as Milton's of that inner liberty; but for Milton, freedom is the government of passion by reason; and when reason reigns among the people, political liberty is secure; when passion has the upper hand, tyranny is inevitable.

"You therefore who wish to remain free, either instantly be wise, or, as soon as possible, cease to

[1] *First Defence*, p. 63.
[2] Ellis, p. 234–235.

be fools; if you think slavery an intolerable evil, learn obedience to reason and the government of yourselves; and finally bid adieu to your dissensions, your jealousies, your superstitions, your outrages, your rapine and your lusts. [1]

Thus both poets looked upon the world of politics from the same point of view. Both were revolutionaries, and vividly interested in the political events of their time.

At the time of the French Revolution, Blake "walked out into the streets of London with a cap of Liberty on his head."[2]

He called himself a "Liberty boy." He consorted with Tom Paine and his friends, and managed to warn Paine in time and save him from prison.[3]

One of Blake's most vigorous—and simple— poems is the first and only remaining canto on *The French Revolution*, an idealistic rendering of the events of 1789, one of the visionary's best things: and it is illuminated by the fullest and most intelligent sympathy with the French Constituants.

The prophecy *America* is much less clear to the non-elect, but has grand passages accessible to all, and is a proof of ardent feeling in favour of the American rebels.

[1] *Second Defence*, p. 299.
[2] Ellis, p. 120.
[3] Ellis, p. 161 and Gilchrist.

But the soberer mind of Milton was prepared to go further than the wildness of Blake. The first bloodshed of the French Revolution made Blake recant and throw away his revolutionary badge[1]. Blake had no sufficient faith in Reason and Ideas to wish them carried out at any cost. Milton was made of sterner stuff and boldly stood up in front of horrified Europe to present the Defence of a King's executioners.

Milton was a man of action and went into the world of men to try to carry out his principles. Blake was content with asserting that

"Empire follows Art, and not vice versa, as Englishmen suppose."[2]

His Imagination was to him more important, more real, than the facts of the world, because he lived essentially in the world of desire. So he charged Milton with being a traitor to the Cause of Imagination:

"Milton was an atheist, busy with this world's affairs till in his old age he returned back to the God he had abandoned in his childhood."[3]

This is wilful misunderstanding of Milton's plans, but fully consistent with Blake's idea that

[1] Ellis, p. 164.
[2] Sampson's edition. *Poems*, p. 141.
[3] Gilchrist, p. 342.

this world is a fabric of Satan's, and therefore the pursuit of all worldly affairs is "atheism."

In spite of these differences, which spring inevitably from the different value of Reason and Desire to each poet, the outlook on politics is practically the same for both.

There is a political side to the great epics of either: *Paradise Lost* was undertaken to

> Justify the ways of God to men,

chiefly in the matter of the Puritans' failure to establish Liberty on this earth, and the conclusion, the XIIth book, is largely political, and finds in the inner degradation of man the cause of all political failure:

> Therefore, since he permits
> Within himself unworthy pow'rs to reign
> Over free reason, God, in judgment just,
> Subjects him from without to violent lords:
> Who oft as undeservedly enthral
> His outward freedom. Tyranny must be;
> Though to the tyrant thereby no excuse.
> Yet, sometimes nations will decline so low
> From virtue (which is reason) that no wrong,
> But justice, and some fatal curse annex'd,
> Deprives them of their outward liberty,
> Their inward lost.[1]

[1] *Paradise Lost*, XII, 90.

One of the meanings of Blake's *Jerusalem*[1] is the symbolical representation of man's political liberation, since

Jerusalem is named Liberty among the Sons of Albion.[2]

That is one of the many keys opening—though none, alas, completely—the secret recesses of Blake's great epic.

Both poets had a similarly exalted idea of England's mission among the nations. Milton boldly enters into the plans of God, and says:

" What does He then but reveal Himself to His servants, and, as His manner is, first to his Englishmen?"[3]

And Blake no less boldly asserts that:

"All things begin and end on Albion's ancient druid rocky shore."[4]

Milton had said:

"Writers of good antiquity and able judgment have been persuaded that even the school of Pythagoras, and the Persian wisdom, took beginning from the old philosophy of this island."[5]

[1] Cf. Berger, p. 350.
[2] *Jerusalem*, p. 26 : illustration.
[3] *Areopagitica*, ed. Garnett, p. 37.
[4] *Jerusalem*, p. 27.
[5] *Aeropagitica* (Bohn), p. 90.

It is to be feared that Milton cannot be acquitted from having here drawn Blake out of his depth into the sea of wild surmises, and is thus partly responsible for much of the English symbolism in Jerusalem, the twelve tribes in England, and Joseph of Arimathea among the rocks of Albion. All symbolical, of course: honi soit qui mal y pense. Still, Blake's lack of precise ideas on historical matters may be somewhat in point also.

In his *Catalogue*, Blake refers to Milton's History of Britain as his covering authority:

Believing with Milton the ancient British history.

but he goes rather farther than his authority, when he says:

"The Britons, say historians, were naked, civilized men, studious, learned, abstruse in thought and contemplation. Adam was a Druid, and Noah also."[1]

This is the work of Imagination which has left Reason behind; and thus far away from Milton is Blake carried, although starting from his grounds —or at least from similar ones.

[1] On the picture "The Ancient Britons."

V. DIFFERENCES

It is necessary to set against these many resemblances between the two poets the principle of all their differences, which, grounded in their views of morality, will often separate them widely in their more abstract conceptions.

Both have the same principle of outside morality, of behaviour: "Fais ce que voudras." But Blake alone has it in the Rabelaisian sense. Blake extends the idea to the inner man. The difference between Blake and Milton is in what each means by the "will." For both, Man is free, and his duty is to do his will. But what is his will?

For Blake, all his desires. All man's wants and passions are holy and are to be followed.

"Those who restrain Desire do so because theirs is weak enough to be restrained; and the restrainer or Reason usurps its place and governs the unwilling."[1]

> Abstinence sows sand all over
> The ruddy limbs and flaming hair,
> But Desire gratified
> Plants fruits of life and beauty there.[2]

Even here Milton partly follows this train of thought: he proclaims the lawfulness of desire.

---

[1] *Marriage of Heaven and Hell.*
[2] *Gnomic Verses*, Sampson, p. 195.

When Blake speaks of an "improvement of sensual enjoyment[1] " he is only enlarging Milton's claims for the sensual life, and vindication of

What God declares pure.[2]

But Milton vindicates what is to him normal desire: desire justified, approved of, led by Reason.

For both poets, the outside morality of man is the same: for both the ideal man will act in the world on the same principle: he follows his will and accepts no law. But the inner morality in each is opposed to the other's. Blake's ideal man will follow his desire, Milton's his reason.

This is the great fundamental difference. We have seen by the religion and the politics of both poets that the difference is more intellectual than practical. But when we turn to their abstract ideas, the gap is wide: the two intellectual systems are largely opposed because of it. Even there great resemblances remain, because practical conceptions have much influence on abstract ideas.

Thus Blake will condemn egoism, and greed and lust of power: and these are at the root of most of the "passions" which Milton condemns. In sex-

[1] *Marriage of Heaven and Hell.*
[2] *Paradise Lost*, IV, 746.

questions, Blake will cry: "Follow pleasure," but
in fact, just as in his life he did not, so in his poems
he abhors "harlots" and "prostitution."

On one practical point however a great difference remains. Blake condemns revenge and
even what we might call justice, whereas Milton
has the fiercest need of both. Milton revels in the
punishments of Hell: at the end of time, both
rebel angels and wicked men shall be sealed up in
the day

Of respiration to the just
And vengeance to the wicked.[1]

And Milton believes in the necessity of atonement for man:

> Die, he or justice must; unless for him
> Some other able, and as willing, pay
> The rigid satisfaction, death for death.[2]

There is the very logic of Justice; Reason im-
movable in practice. And this is abhorrent to
Blake. It is one of the cardinal errors for him to
think

"That God will torment Man in Eternity for
following his Desires."[3]

---

[1] *Paradise Lost*, XII, 540.
[2] *Paradise Lost*, III, 210.
[3] *Marriage of Heaven and Hell.*

He proclaims that:

> Mutual forgiveness of each vice
> Such are the Gates of Paradise.[1]

The Saviour, Christ, has created the limits of
contraction, so that none can go beyond them and
be utterly lost; at the end of *Jerusalem* Jesus comes
to bring forgiveness and reconciliation to all:

> So Jesus spoke; the Covering cherub coming on in
>   darkness
> Overshadow'd them and Jesus said: Thus do Men in
>   Eternity,
> One for another to put off, by forgiveness, every sin.[2]

Blake hated the idea of atonement.
Crabb Robinson reports:[3]

"He spoke of atonement. Said: It is a horrible
doctrine. If another man pay your debt, I do not
forgive it."

This is a great difference between Blake and
Milton's ideas. But in spite of it, in fact, their
temperament was the same: Blake's language
against his offending friends was as uncontrolled
and as virulent as Milton's against his foes.

[1] *The Gates of Paradise.*
[2] *Jerusalem* p 96.
[3] *Diary*, Symons, p. 271.

Thus morality has presented to Blake and Milton the same problem: the struggles between desire and reason. They have solved it in reverse ways; so that Blake is intellectually a sort of inverted Milton.

The difference is great between them in the world of imagination and intellect. But in the world of fact, their characters, which put the same problem to them, were in many things similar, with less self-control, perhaps simply more wilfulness, in Blake. And as there is much passion in Milton, the apostle of Reason, so there is much reason in Blake, the champion of Passion.

Hence their peculiar relationship, in similarity and difference, which makes the study of either a light for the understanding of the other.

CHAPTER IV

THE FALL AND THE NORMAL STATE

I. GENERAL VIEW OF THE FALL

THE account of the Fall is as simple and clear in Milton as it is complex, and, at first sight at least, obscure in Blake. Apparently, the two conceptions are quite opposed. But the opposition is more a question of vocabulary and imagery than of ideas.

Milton thus describes the State of Fall:

> Understanding ruled not, and the will
> Heard not her lore, both in subjection now
> To sensual appetite, who from beneath
> Usurping over sovereign reason claimed
> Superior sway.[1]

And Adam has been accordingly represented as allowing his passion to triumph over his reason:

> Against his better knowledge, not deceived,
> But fondly overcome by female charm.[2]

[1] *Paradise Lost*, IX, 1128.   [2] IX, 998.

Among the many accounts of the Fall given by Blake, the most consistent, the one oftenest referred to, runs somewhat as follows:

The Eternal Man—the One Great Being—lived in peace and inner harmony. But War broke out between Urizen, who is Intellect, and Luvah, who is Passion, each wanting to gain mastery over the whole man. The Eternal man's family

Slept round on hills and valleys in the region of his
    love,
But Urizen awoke, and Luvah awoke, and they
    conferred, thus:

(Urizen proposes a division of man between him and Luvah)[1]—

               "Deep in the North I place my Lot
Thou in the South. Listen attentive. In silence of this
    night
I will infold the universal tent in clouds opaque, while
    thou
Seizest the chariots of the morning. Go; outfleeing
    ride
Afar into the Zenith high, bending thy furious course
Towards the South."—
Luvah replied: "Dictate thou to thy equals, am I not
The Prince of all the hosts of men, nor equal know
    in Heaven?

[1] *Vala*, I, 445.

If I arise into the Zenith, leaving thee to watch,
— — wilt thou not, rebel to my laws, remain
In darkness, building thy strong throne, and in my
    ancient night
Daring my power wilt arm my sons against me in the
    deep,
My deep, my night, which thou assuming hast assumed
    my crown."

A terrible combat ensues, then Urizen departs
towards the North,

                Leaving the rage of Luvah
To pour its fury on himself and on the Eternal Man.

But the Eternal Man calls upon Urizen to take
possession of him; then,

Luvah was cast into the furnaces of affliction and
    sealed.[1]

And he laments thus:

                "I suffer affliction
Because I love, for I was Love, but hatred awakes in
    me
And Urizen who was Faith and certainty is changed to
    Doubt,

  [1] *Vala*, II, 70.

The hand of Urizen is upon me—
        Oh first born son of Light
Oh, Urizen, my enemy, I weep for thy stern
    ambition."[1]

Then Urizen builds this World, and his laws;
and Man's submission to Him is the state of the
Fall.

Scattered allusions through the poems apprise
us that Urizen had allowed his horses to be led by
Luvah:

Why didst thou listen to the voice of Luvah that dread
    morn
To give the immortal steeds of light to his deceitful
    hands.[2]

The simplest explanation of this complicated
myth is that the Fall is the domination of Intellect
over Desire; and such is, no doubt, the general idea
of Blake, as clearly expressed in the *Marriage of
Heaven and Hell*. This is directly opposed to
Milton's view.

But Blake's meaning is much more complex;
and its complications and qualifications bring it
very near to the Miltonic theories.

First of all, Urizen seems, before the Fall, to have

---

[1] *Vala*, II, 99.   [2] *Vala*, III, 32.

held a sort of supremacy. That is why Luvah calls
him the first born Prince of Light. But then
Urizen in the State of Harmony was not pure
Intellect[1]: he was Reason vivified by Feeling,
mixed with Imagination. Blake proclaims thus
the necessity of Feeling to the proper working of
Reason; as he does when he writes:

(Messiah: i.e. Reason) "prays to the Father to
send the Comforter, or Desire, that Reason may
have Ideas to build on."[2]

But Urizen wished to reign alone. He fails, and
then Luvah, Passion, reigns over man. Man is torn
by inner wars. This is quite Miltonic in thought:
the reign of Passion is evil. The Eternal man,
unable to bear it, calls to Urizen to take power over
him. Here Blake is still in agreement with Milton:
Reason should triumph. But Blakes pursues the
myth further.

Urizen coming back to reign over the Eternal
Man is no longer Inspired Intelligence ; he has
separated from feeling. He is the logical power,
essentially the maker of Laws and of Religions.
And Milton, as we have seen, is as much as Blake
the enemy of Law and Religions.

The mode of Intellect which Milton wishes to

---

[1] Cf. Ellis and Yeats, vol I, p. 267.
[2] *The Marriage of Heaven and Hell.*

reign over man is not therefore the Fallen Urizen, mechanical Intellect, but the primitive and glorious Zoa, in which Imagination, Feeling and Reason were united.

Thus only a question of vocabulary separates the two poets on this important point. By intellect, Blake means a maimed sort of Intelligence, a mechanical law-making activity, which was as repellent to Milton as to Blake himself. By Reason Milton means an exalted form of intellectual power, mainly fed by divine Inspiration; and in many ways similar to the " Imagination " which Blake wanted to see dominant.

In their conception of the Normal State and in their conception of the Fall the two poets come very near each other, because their ideas sprang from similar temperaments and similar experiences. Only Blake's wilder imagination complicated the original myth past recognition, and he himself posed then as a spiritual enemy of Milton. In this attitude his pride had a large part, and the wilfulness which prevented him from studying precisely the meaning of any one author, and led him to judge other minds by his first intuitions, often intuitions of genius, as often pure imaginings of the visionary.

In many points of detail the similarity of Blake's

and Milton's view is obvious. The error, often alluded to, of Urizen allowing Luvah to lead his horses, is the origin of the Fall: and it can mean nothing but the domination of Intellect by Desire.

Blake's mind was singularly well balanced under all his extravagances: He recognized that Passion ought no more to triumph over Reason than inversely Intellect over Desire. He proclaimed the necessity of harmony inside man, in the full exercise of all his faculties.

The Fall is for him the estrangement of the powers of man from each other, much more than the domination of this or that power. Thus Blake reaches—or allows us to reach when we read him— a very large conception of the human soul: in which he wishes to suppress nothing, seeing the fundamental and essential unity and necessity of all its manifestations.

And this conception was Milton's since Milton vindicated the legitimacy of all normal desires of man, recognizing the essential goodness of matter and of the body,

> Whatever hypocrites austerely talk
> Of purity and place and innocence,
> Defaming as impure what God declares
> Pure, and commands to some, leaves free to all.[1]

[1] *Paradise Lost*, IV, 744.

There are thus many resemblances between the two poets, in the moral impulse which is at the basis of their conception of the Fall. But in the intellectual working out of this vein, differences develop. Milton's normal desire is only recognized as normal when sanctioned by Reason. Raphael instructs Adam:

> In loving thou dost well, in passion not
> Wherein true love consists not: love refines
> The thoughts, and heart enlarges, has his seat
> In Reason, and is judicious.[1]

But Blake holds that:

"Those who restrain Desire, do so because theirs is weak enough to be restrained—it by degrees becomes passive, till it is only the shadow of Desire."[2]

And Blake has summed up the differences between his and Milton's views of the Fall:

"But the Devil's account is, that the Messiah fell, and formed a Heaven of what he stole from the Abyss."[3]

Thus Urizen—Intellect—falls; and builds the world of Law upon what remains to him of the life-stuff of the Eternal Man. This conception is

[1] *Paradise Lost*, V, 587.
[2] *Marriage of Heaven and Hell.*

present through the whole Blakean description of the Fall, and weaves the woof of the differences upon the warp of resemblances with the Miltonic view.

Besides, Blake has many different accounts, and several different interpretations of the Fall, and they often blend together, to the perplexity of the reader. And he is not always coherent in his use of names. In *The Marriage of Heaven and Hell:* Satan is Passion, and Blake his prophet. In *Milton*

Los and Enitharmon knew that Satan is Urizen.

That is to say, Intellect in its destructive form, Blake's great enemy. And in *Jerusalem*, in the lyrical myth enacted in

The fields from Islington to Marylebone.[1]

Satan is the Rational Power, which causes the Fall by his enterprise.

Besides, in *Jerusalem*, the hero of which is chiefly Los, the Inspired Prophet, it seems that the Power which must not be expelled is Imagination, rather than feeling; the two antagonists: Reason and Desire, seemingly becoming Reason and Imagination. This may be simply the peculiar form of the

[1] P. 27.

Fall proper to Loss, as each Zoa, and perhaps each character in the *Prophetic Books* has its own particular way of coming to grief, when its Emanation separates from its Spectre.

All these complexities take us further and further from Milton's clear and reasonable account of the Fall. And it is as a thread of light in tumultuous darkness when occasionally we catch a Miltonic trait, as when we are told that

> Men are caught by Love: Woman is caught by Pride.[1]

and we remember the history of Adam following his beloved into perdition open-eyed, and Eve enticed to her loss by Satan's flattery.

In the two accounts of Man's regeneration, the resemblances are few in the elaborate detail work. The general idea, balancing the chief idea of the Fall, is that Harmony is re-established in Man; and in this Blake and Milton agree, just as they disagree, superficially at least, as to what that re-established harmony is.

However, we are told in *Vala* that Urizen is the first Power to be regenerated, and the Eternal

[1] *Jerusalem*, p. 81.

Man gives him power over Passions and Desires. This is quite in harmony with Milton's ideas:

And now fierce Orc had quite consumed himself in
    mental flames,
Expending all his energy against the fuel of the fire.
The Regenerate Man stooped his holy head over the
    universe, and in
His holy hands received the flaming demon and dim-
    ness of smoke
And gave him to Urizen's hands. The immortal
    frowned, saying:
Luvah and Vala, henceforth you are servants, obey and
    live.[1]

So Intellect, although in a transfigured Form, which would however have been quite acceptable to Milton, after all reigns over Desire.

In the Regeneration, Blake insists that:

Every man is king and priest in his own house.[2]

and this is again a Miltonic feature in the Blakean chaos.

One metaphysical aspect of the Regeneration common to both poets is the Union of the Elect in Jesus; but this has no bearing upon the moral

---

[1] *Vala*, IX, 354.
[2] Quoted by Ellis and Yeats, vol. I, p. 286.

relationship between Blake and Milton, and is rather in connection with their pantheism. It will find its place accordingly in the study of the poets' common metaphysics.

II. SEX AND SENSUALITY

In close connection with the two poets' moral views and their ideas of the Fall and Regeneration stands their conception of Sex and the part Sex plays in man's life.

Crabb Robinson relates that Blake spoke of Milton thus:[1]

"I have seen him as a youth and as an old man with a long, flowing beard. He came lately as an old man—he said he came to ask a favour of me. He said he had committed an error in his *Paradise Lost*, which he wanted me to correct, in a poem or a picture. But I declined. I said I had my own duties to perform.

"He wished me to expose the falsehood of his doctrine taught in the *Paradise Lost*, that sexual intercourse arose out of the Fall. Now that cannot be, for no good can spring out of evil."

This is, as usual with Blake, a mixture of intuition, wilfulness and error.

Milton certainly held that lust arose out of the

[1] *Diary*, Symons, p. 295.

Fall; but then he distinguished between lust and a permissible sensuality which he admits in his Paradise and is strong in praise of. Therefore he does not make good spring out of evil. He makes the Fall pervert sensuality.

On the other hand, Blake himself was at times much more thorough-going than Milton and condemned all sensuality, and the very existence of Sex, as an allurement drawing souls into this life, which is bad.

And yet the general spirit of Blake's remark is true in this way, that Blake as a rule spoke strongly in praise and in favour of Desire, hence often of sensuality. But then again, so did Milton.

On the whole, it can be said that both poets are fairly at one on the question of sensuality. Both give to the facts of sensual life, and then to woman generally, a most important place in their scheme of Life. This, of course, comes from a similar passionate temperament, and is in harmony with the important part played by woman in the two poets' lives. Both, from a certain point of view, claim the legitimacy and the necessity of the satisfaction of sensual desire. Yet, from another point of view, both see the Fall in Sensuality, and Blake even in Sex. And as a consequence, they have a similar conception of the part of woman in man's life.

Differences occur in points of detail. They come generally from a lack of a precise standard in Blake's mind for judging the facts of Sex: Milton had his clear theory of Reason: when Reason is at one with Desire, when the union of man and woman includes mind and heart, then sensuality is good. But Blake repudiated the judgment of Reason; therefore he is often contradictory, for he had an instinct of purity as strong as Milton's, but often knew not how to justify it.

When Blake speaks of "Desire," he often means simply sensual desire. Many of his lyrics run on that subject, and some of his most penetrating ones:

> I laid me down upon a bank
> Where Love lay sleeping;
> I heard among the rushes dank
> Weeping, weeping.
>
> Then I went to the heath and the wild,
> To the thistles and thorns of the waste;
> And they told me how they were beguil'd,
> Driven out and compell'd to be chaste.

A Little Girl Lost, celebrates pure youthful pleasure, in a tone worthy of Milton's own description of Love in the Golden age of Paradise:

Children of the future age,
Reading this indignant page,
Know that in a former clime
Love, sweet love, was thought a crime.

In the age of gold, free from winter's cold,
Youth and maiden bright,
To the holy light,
Naked in the sunny beams delight.

Once a youthful pair,
Fill'd with softest care,
Met in garden bright,
Where the holy light
Had just removed the curtains of the night.

For purity and delicacy of feeling such lyrics are only matched perhaps in Milton.

Nor turn'd I ween,
Adam from his fair spouse, nor Eve the rites
Mysterious of connubial love refused—
—These, lulled by nightingales, embracing slept
And on their naked limbs the flowery roof
Showered roses.

Both poets vindicate a cause, are up in arms against puritanical enemies, are not only lyrical, but argumentative:

¹ *Paradise Lost*, IV, 741, 771.

Blake sings:

Infancy! Fearless, lustful, happy, nestling for delight
In laps of pleasure: Innocence! honest, open, seeking
The vigorous joys of morning light, open to virgin
    bliss,
Who taught thee modesty, subtil modesty, child of
    night and sleep?
When thou awakest wilt thou dissemble all thy secret
    joys?[1]

And Milton thunders against hypocrisy on the
same subject:

Whatever hypocrites austerely talk
Of purity and place and innocence,
Defaming as impure what God declares
Pure, and commands to some, leaves free to all.
Our Maker bids increase, who bids abstain
But our Destroyer, foe to God and man?
—Far be it, that I should write thee sin or blame
Or think thee unbefitting holiest place,
Perpetual fountain of domestic sweets,
Whose bed is undefiled and chaste pronounced,
Present, or past, as saints and patriarchs used.[2]

Thus far, both Blake and Milton are at one. But
Milton needs must explain his feeling more pre-

---

[1] *Visions of the Daughters of Albion*, 156.
[2] *Paradise Lost*, IV, 742–762.

cisely; nowhere so precisely as in his Divorce
tracts, where he speaks as follows of physical love:

"Although (it) be considered among the ends
of marriage, yet the act thereof in a right esteem
can no longer be matrimonial, than it is an effect
of conjugal love—proceeding as it ought from
intellective principles, it participates of (the)
rational." "If the body do out of sensitive force
what the soul complies not with, how can man,
and not rather something beneath man, be thought
the doer."[1]

Hence Milton's hymn is to wedded Love,
"founded in reason," like the "charities" that
come from it, for Love

> has his seat
> In reason, and is judicious[2] :

Hail, wedded love! mysterious law, true source
Of human offspring, sole propriety
In Paradise of all things common else.
By thee adulterous lust was driven from men
Among the bestial herds to range; by thee,
Founded in reason, loyal, just and pure,
Relations dear, and all the charities
Of father, son and brother, first were known.[3]

[1] *Tetrachordon*, p. 342.
[2] *Paradise Lost*, V, 589.
[3] *Paradise Lost*, IV, 750.

But here Blake can no longer follow. His Desire must be free: he will admit neither the control of reason, as we have seen him write often, nor the "sole propriety." He cries:

Father of Jealousy, be thou accursed from the earth!
Why hast thou taught my Theotormon this accursed
    thing,
Till beauty fades from off my shoulders, darken'd and
    cast out,
A solitary shadow wailing on the margin of nonentity?

I cry: Love! Love! Love! happy, happy Love! free as
    the mountain wind!
Can that be Love, that drinks another as a sponge
    drinks water[1]?

And the liberty which he demands for women by the voice of Oothoon he demands for men by the action of Milton himself. And it is true that Milton did look favourably upon polygamy,[2]—although the alternate part of Blake's creed of freedom he would have strongly objected to:

And the Divine Voice was heard in the songs of
    Beulah, saying:

---

[1] *Visions of the Daughters of Albion*, 187.
[2] Cf. *Treatise of Christian Doctrine*, p. 225 to 237.

When I first married you, I gave you all my whole
    soul,
I thought that you would love my loves and joy in my
    delights,
Seeking for pleasures in my pleasures, o daughter of
    Babylon[1]
Then thou wast lovely, mild and gentle, now thou
    art terrible
In Jealousy, and unlovely in my sight, because thou
    hast cruelly
Cut off my Loves in fury, till I have no Love left for
    thee.

When the Sixfold Female perceives that Milton
    annihilates
Himself, that seeing all his loves cut off, he leaves
Her also, entirely abstracting himself from Female
    loves,
She shall relent in fear of death; she shall begin to give
Her maidens to her husband, and delight in his delight.[1]

Milton did not venture so far in his poems. But
he devoted pages of his *Treatise on Christian Doctrine*
to a justification of polygamy.[2]

In reality, there was in both men too much purity
and too much kindness of heart to carry their
ideas into practice. Blake was stopped by his wife's

[1] *Milton*, f. 32.
[2] P. 225 to 237.

tears from introducing a "handmaiden" into his home; and Milton took back his repentant weeping wife without inflicting any such humiliation upon her.

As Blake had known jealousy,[1] and was not the man to follow his ideas when his feelings opposed, it seems highly probable that his views of sensual liberty for women would have remained also purely theoretical.

So that really the only point that remains at issue between the two poets is the idea of Reason, for Blake held to the last that

The Negation is the Spectre, the Reasoning Power in
    man.[2]

III. SENSUALITY AS THE FALL

Milton makes of sensuality the first, and essential, manifestation of the Fall:

> They swim in mirth, and fancy that they feel
> Divinity within them breeding wings
> Wherewith to scorn the earth; but that false fruit
> Far other operation first displayed
> Carnal desire inflaming; he on Eve
> Began to cast lascivious eyes, she him
> As wantonly repaid; in lust they burn.[3]

[1] Cf. Ellis, p. 37–38.   [2] *Milton*, p. 42.
[3] *Paradise Lost*, IX, 1009.

The Fall, understood in the narrow sense of the word is Lust—Lust is the essential expression of the larger Fall: the triumph of passion over reason. Adam discerns:

> In our faces evident the signs
> Of foul concupiscence;[1]

because

> Understanding ruled not, and the will
> Heard not her lore, both in subjection now
> To sensual appetite.[2]

Blake has a horror of debauchery which is as marked as Milton's and with a sort of mystical awe added, as before an incomprehensible and terrible power of evil; he writes in his rhymed proverbs with the fierceness of an old prophet:

> The harlot's cry from street to street
> Shall weave old England's winding sheet.

His vision of *London* in the *Songs of Experience* ends on the same note:

> But most thro' midnight streets I hear
> How the youthful harlot's curse
> Blasts the new-born infant's tear,
> And blights with plagues the marriage hearse.

[1] *Paradise Lost*, IX, 1078.
[2] *Paradise Lost*, IX, 1127.

And whoever and whatever "The Shadowy Female" of the *Prophetic Books* may be, her cry is "the harlot's cry," and Orc, "her only beloved" seems to be an impersonation of physical passion:

My garments shall be woven of sighs and heart-broken
    lamentations.
The misery of unhappy families shall be drawn out
    into its border,
Wrought with the needle, with dire sufferings,
    poverty, pain and woe.—
—And all my ornaments shall be of the gold of broken
    hearts
And the precious stones of anxiety and care, and
    desperation and death
And repentance for sin and sorrow, and punishment
    and fear,
To defend me from thy terrors, O Orc, my only
    beloved.[1]

Blake lacks the clear distinction of Milton between normal desire, approved of by reason, and good, and evil lust, the Fall. His general thesis of "Unreason" keeps him from that solution. He has the two Miltonic elements: glorification of physical love, and horror of debauchery, but he fails to give us a clear differentiation. It is with

[1] *Milton*, p. 17.

him a question of feeling chiefly, the natural purity
of his soul asserting itself alongside of his theories.
But the result is not always clear, and such characters as Oothoon, and such poems as the *Visions of
the Daughters of Albion* leave a disturbing and
somewhat unhealthy impression.

So sensuality plays a large part in Blake's conception of the Fall, and, inconsistently enough,
much the same part as in Milton's: whether
Blake, for all his having refused to do or to undo
Milton's work, was deeply influenced by him, or
whether the similarities of temperament in the two
poets were simply having their natural effect.

This is one of the accounts of the Fall in *Vala*.
Enitharmon speaks:

> Now listen, I will tell
> The secrets of Eternity which ne'er before unlocked
> My golden lips, nor took the bar from Enitharmon's
>   breast;
> Among the flowers of Beulah walked the Eternal Man
>   and saw
> Vala, the lily of the desert. Melting in high noon
> Upon her bosom in sweet bliss he fainted. Wonder seized
> All Heaven for they saw him dark. They built a
>   golden wall
> Round Beulah. There he revelled in delight among
>   the flowers.

Vala was pregnant and brought forth Urizen, Prince
    of Light,
First born of Generation. Then a wonder to the eyes
Of the now fallen man, a double form Vala appeared,
    a male
And female shuddering. Pale at sight the fallen man
    recoiled,
Down vales to find his way back into heaven, but
    found none
And calling the Enormity Luvah and Vala, turned
For his frail eyes were faded, and his ears heavy and
    dull.[1]

This is a weaving of many Miltonic threads,
among others. The Eternal Man walking among
the flowers and meeting Vala is reminiscent of the
first meeting of Adam and Eve. The revelling in
delight among the flowers is a concentration of the
Miltonic sensual fall:

            Flowers were the couch,
     Pansies and violets and asphodels,
     And hyacinth, earth's freshest, softest lap.[2]

The intricate births of the Zoas from each other
recall Satan's progeny of Sin and Death in the
Miltonic allegory. And the Eternal man, fallen,
who tried

---

[1] *Vala*, night VII, 234.   [2] *Paradise Lost*, IX, 1039.

to find his way back into Heaven, but found none

is a good counterpart of Adam after the Fall.

But the chief thing is the central idea. Sensuality is represented as the Fall, and the sexes "shuddering" seem in turn to arise out of the Fall.

This is borne out by the general character of Vala and Luvah in the *Prophetic Books*. Vala represents chiefly sexual attraction[1] and Luvah is Passion generally. In the State of Fall, Luvah is dominant in man, as against Urizen, alternately triumphant; and Vala seeks dominion:

The Fallen man takes his repose, Urizen slept in the porch,
Luvah and Vala wake up and fly up from the Human Heart
Into the Brain.[2]

This seems like a translation into some unknown mythology of Milton's

For understanding ruled not, and the will
Heard not her lore, both in subjection now
To sensual appetite.

Then Blake rises higher, and identifies sensuality

[1] Cf. Ellis and Yeats, vol. I, p. 280; Berger, p. 149.
[2] *Vala*, I, 238.

and the Fall, on a cosmic plane. The division into sexes is the Fall, or the first effect of it:

You become Mortal and Vegetable in Sexuality.[1]

Vala becomes "Nature in her sensual beauty, ever weaving her veil or net to catch the souls,"[2] that is to say, to entice unborn beings into this world, which Blake calls death. Sensuality is the cause of births; and Birth is the Fall of a soul into this world, which is evil: matter and physical bodies are evil; and physical love entagles free souls into matter. Hence the poem to Tirzah, who is Physical Nature, or perhaps Motherhood:

> Whatever is born of mortal birth,
> Must be consumed with the earth
> To rise from generation free;
> Then what have I to do with thee?
> Thou, Mother of my mortal part,
> With cruelty didst mould my heart,
> And with false self-deceiving tears,
> Didst bind my nostrils, eyes and ears,
>
> Didst close my tongue in senseless clay,
> And me to mortal life betray—.

[1] *Milton*, p. 35, l. 24.
[2] Russell and Maclagan, Preface to *Jerusalem*, p. xi.

Thus following upon this new idea, Blake makes of material beauty, of Nature, of Love, fatal things. Milton had made of matter "the source of all subsequent good." But Blake had no test to tell him how far to go in his condemnation of sensuality: therefore he went, while in the mood, much further than Milton, and banned to perdition the whole material world. In a similar, but contrary way, when in the opposite mood, he would admit of no restriction to sensuality. In both directions he followed Miltonic tendencies, but his enmity to Reason deprived him of the Miltonic test of the harmony between Desire and Intelligence. So in both directions, careless of contradiction, he pushed his ideas to their utmost bourne.

IV.   VIEWS OF WOMAN

However complicated those intellectual resemblances and differences, when it comes to real facts, Milton and Blake are most often at one. And so they agree in their view of woman.

Crabb Robinson says of Catherine Blake:

"She was formed on the Miltonic model, and like the first Wife, Eve, worshipped God in her husband. He being to her what God was to him."[1]

[1] Crabb Robinson Ed. Symons, p. 294.

As Blake had shaped the pliable nature of his wife into his ideal, this was then to him the right conception of woman:

He for God only, she for God in him.[1]

For both poets, man is predominant; woman being only the softer, weaker side of him.

This is all the more characteristic of Blake, since all his feminine "Emanations" represent Desire as distinct from the hard logic of the "Spectres" from which they separate. And according to his general idea Desire ought to predominate in Man.

On the contrary, for Blake as for Milton, the leadership of Woman is the source of all evil. Milton begins at the Fall, when Adam was induced to his perdition by Eve, and carries it on through the whole of life:

> Therefore God's universal law
> Gave to the man despotic power
> Over his female in due awe,
> Nor from that right to part an hour
> Smile she or lower—
> So shall he least confusion draw
> On his whole life, not swayed
> By female usurpation, or dismayed.[2]

[1] *Paradise Lost*, IV, 299.
[2] *Samson Agonistes*, 1052.

Blake is no less categorical:

There is a throne in every man, it is the Throne of
    God
This Woman has claim'd as her own, and Man is no
    more!
Albion is the tabernacle of Vala and her Temple
And not the Tabernacle and Temple of the Most
    High.[1]

But though both give to woman a subordinate
position, both have a very high idea of her. Man
cannot do without her. She represents the gentler
and lovelier side of his nature, and he is maimed
and incomplete without her: his superiority
becoming then barren and unbearable. Woman
is essentially different from man, and fills a gap in
his nature.

Milton writes in the *Tetrachordon:*

"No mortal nature can endure, either in the
actions of religion or study of wisdom, without
sometime slackening the cords of intense thought
and labour, which, lest we should think faulty,
God himself conceals us not his own recreations,
before the world was built: "I was," saith the
Eternal Wisdom, "daily his delight, playing always
before him." And to him indeed wisdom is as a

[1] *Jerusalem.*

high tower of pleasure, but to us a steep hill and we toiling ever about the bottom. He executes with ease the exploits of his omnipotence, as easy as for us it is to will; but no worthy enterprise can be done by us without continual plodding and wearisomeness to our faint and sensitive abilities. We cannot therefore always be contemplative or pragmatical abroad, but have need of some delightful intermissions, wherein the enlarged soul may leave off a while her severe schooling, and, like a glad youth in wandering vacancy, may keep her holidays to joy and harmless pastime; which as she cannot do well without company, so in no company so well as where the different sex in most resembling unlikeness, and most unlike resemblance, cannot but please best, and be pleased in the aptitude of that variety."[1]

The trends of thought embodied in this page are all important in Blake's conception of life. All these feelings of Milton exist in Blake, expressed differently, and playing an essential part in his system. Not that he was directly inspired by the passage: his expression is much too far from it. But the same feelings prompted him to similar ideas. The same feelings led Blake to his theory of the Emanations.

[1] *Tetrachordon*, p. 331 (Bohn, III).

The Emanation is the soft emotional side of a being; the female part. Without her he is in a state of unnatural tension and hardness, harsh, logical, inhuman. Blake evolves the conception of that part of man which would never slacken, in the actions of religion, or the study of wisdom, the cords of intense thought and labour, into the ghostly image of the "Spectre."

A Negation,
Not only of the Substance from which it is derived,
A murderer of its own body: but also a murderer
Of every divine member: it is the Reasoning power,
This is the Spectre of Man: the Holy Reasoning
    power.[1]

It frames Laws and Moralities
To destroy Imagination, the Divine Body.[2]

The ultimate picture is far enough from Milton; but the starting point is Milton's. The necessity of a softer spirit as a companion to man, the necessity of woman.

And it is a similar process which makes both poets sublimate this notion, and give to the softer spirit an immense metaphysical and cosmological importance:

[1] *Jerusalem*, p. 10.   [2] *Jerusalem*, p. 74.

Milton imagining feminine powers in the very existence of God before Creation, delighting Him by their play; and Blake making of his Spectre and Emanation principles of universal explanation.

Thus after all with both poets woman comes into her own as an indispensable power; one without which man cannot exist; one concerned in the very making and vivifying of the Universe.

By both poets, woman is conceived as the instrument and the vase of Passion: necessary in itself, but not to be dominant. Milton evolves from that point of view a well balanced and reasonable theory as to woman's place, acknowledging yet by Adam's voice that

> All higher knowledge in her presence falls
> Degraded; wisdom in discourse with her
> Loses discountenanced, and like folly shows:
> Authority and reason on her wait,
> As one intended first, not after made,
> Occasionally.[1]

Blake, with whom Passion is free, exalts higher still the role of woman. Although he represents her also as a part, and a submissive part, of man, yet he makes man more needful of her. Without their Emanations, all beings fall into a state of

[1] *Paradise Lost*, VIII, 551.

perdition, the tales of the horrors of which fill the *Prophetic Books*. And the final Redemption of Man can only be accomplished by the re-instauration of the Emanation as a leading power in each particular Being, and the destruction of the Spectre :

> Each man is in his Spectre's power,
> Untill the arrival of that hour
> When his humanity awake
> And cast his Spectre into the Lake.[1]

And the tale of the Zoas and their Emanations is none other than the transposed poor human tale of Adam and Eve as told by Milton: the Emanation tempts the Being to some act which is thereafter considered as Sin by both; then she is repudiated by him; and laments, and begs to be taken back; and ultimately she is taken back into his Love and cherished again; and both are strong and regenerated.

Milton has told the tale simply and with effective art: Adam soon began his repudiation of Eve:

> O Eve, in evil hour didst thou give ear
> To that false worm—[2]

[1] Motto to *Jerusalem*.
[2] *Paradise Lost*, IX, 1067.

And of their vain contest appeared no end;

And Eve first sought reconciliation, to be denounced all the more bitterly:

> Soft words to his fierce passion she assayed[1];
> But her with stern regard he thus repelled:
> Out of my sight, thou serpent—.

But she desisted not:

> While yet we live, scarce one short hour perhaps,
> Between us two let there be peace—

And it is the first step of Regeneration when she prevails, and Man is again at peace within himself, saying to his wife:

> —let us no more contend, nor blame
> Each other.[2]

Blake transports this simple theme into the wild world of his Imagination; but his underlying feeling is of the bitterness of contention between man and woman—derived from his own experience, even as Milton's; and the fundamental traits, behind all Blake's metaphysical abstractions,

[1] *Paradise Lost*, X, from 862 onwards.
[2] *Paradise Lost*, X, 958.

those which touch us deeply are the sensitive human traits, the real feelings of our common humanity, which after all are the basis of the whole Blakean edifice :

As Adam, Urizen speaks to Ahania, his Emanation:

> Thus I cast thee out:
> Shall the feminine indolent bliss, the indulgent self of weariness
> Set herself up to give her laws to this active masculine virtue.
> —Wherefore hast thou taken this fair form?
> Whence is this power given thee? Once thou wast in my breast,
> A sluggish current of dim waters, on whose verdant margin
> I laid my head in the hot noon, after the broken clods
> Had wearied me—
> And thou hast risen with thy moist locks into a watery image
> Reflecting all my indolence, my weakness and my death.[1]

For the First Sin has been committed through the Feminine Power:

[1] *Vala*, III, 114, etc.

Dire shriek'd his invisible Lust[1]
Deep groan'd Urizen—
He groan'd, anguished, and call'd her Sin,
Kissing her and weeping over her—

She fell down, a faint Shadow, wandering
In Chaos.—

But the Emanation, like Eve, attempts reconciliation, and approaches her Master with soft
words:

Creature so fair his reconcilement seeking:
                    Ah! Urizen! Love!
Flower of morning! I weep on the verge
Of Nonentity—how wide the Abyss
Between Ahania and thee!
Why didst thou despise Ahania,
To cast me from thy bright presence,
Into the World of Loneness?[2]

When wilt thou return and view
My loves and them to life renew?
When wilt thou return and live?
When wilt thou pity as I forgive?

O'er my sins thou sit and moan:
Hast thou no sins of thy own?[3]

[1] Urizen's *Book of Ahania*, chap. I, 7.
[2] *The Book of Ahania*, ch. V.
[3] *My Spectre around me Night and Day*, Sampson 130.

And it is truer in Blake than in Milton that

Of their vain contest appeared no end.

But even in Blake things come to an end, and the end is also reconciliation: and Albion, the Eternal Man, at last calls to his Emanation, Jerusalem:

Awake, Awake Jerusalem! O lovely Emanation of
    Albion,
For lo! the night of death is past and the Eternal Day
Appears upon our Hills: Awake, Jerusalem and come
    away![1]

And at that time :

Bright Ahania took her seat by Urizen in songs and
    joy.[2]

[1] *Jerusalem*, 97.
[2] *Vala*, IX, 349.

CHAPTER V

METAPHYSICAL IDEAS

I. METHODS OF THOUGHT: INSPIRATION, DOGMA, REVELATION

BLAKE and Milton came to metaphysical questions with much the same intellectual methods. Both believed in Divine Inspiration as a direct source of knowledge in themselves and in all great men; both considered all settled dogma as merely figurative, a symbol to be interpreted; both looked upon the Bible in the same way: as a book inspired by God more directly than others, though not as the Unique Book of Revelation; nor even as exempt from error, but indeed as far below the direct inspiration of the poet himself.

Milton clearly puts down his idea that all great poets, whatever time or nation they belong to, are directly inspired by God:

"These abilities, wheresoever they be found, are the inspired gift of God, rarely bestowed, but yet to some (though most abuse) in every nation."[1]

[1] *Reason of Church Government*, Bohn, vol II, p. 479.

In the *Areopagitica:* he speaks of Spenser "whom I dare be known to think a better teacher than Scotus or Aquinas."[1]

Blake has a similarly high idea of the poets' mission. His Los is, from some points of view, a personification of the poetic Spirit:

Therefore the Sons of Eden praise Urthona's Spectre
    in songs,
Because he kept the divine vision in times of trouble.[2]

And Los-Urthona has inspired all poets and prophets for the liberation of mankind. Writing in another language, Blake asks:

"Is the Holy Ghost any other than an Intellectual fountain?"[3]

Conceiving every great man to be inspired, Blake could do justice even to his enemies: Crabb Robinson relates:

"He understood the Bible in a Spiritual sense. As to the natural sense, he said Voltaire was commissioned by God to expose that. "I have had," he said, "much intercourse with Voltaire, and he said to me : 'I blasphemed the Son of Man, and it shall be forgiven me, but they (the enemies of

---

[1] *Areopagitica* (Garnett, p. 15).
[2] *Jerusalem*, p. 95.
[3] *Jerusalem*, p. 27.

Voltaire) blasphemed the Holy Ghost in me, and it shall not be forgiven them.'"[1]

Blake went farther on that road, although even then he only developed Miltonic ideas.

Blake reports his conversations with Ezekiel and Isaiah:

"We of Israel taught that the Poetic Genius was the First Principle—and that all Gods would at last be proved to originate in ours and to be tributaries of the Poetic Genius."[2]

And Blake goes on to a theory of the origin of all religions, by which his theory of inspiration merges into his pantheism:

"The ancient Poets animated all sensible objects with Gods or Geniuses—thus men forgot that all Deities reside in the human breast."[3]

"The worship of God: Honouring his gifts in other men, each according to his genius, and loving the greatest men best; those who envy or calumniate great men hate God, for there is no other God."[4]

All this sounds Voltarian enough, but really it is only Miltonic. It is only Milton's theory that "all of us are of God,"[5] being made of the primeval

[1] *Diary* (Symons), p. 301.   [5] *Marriage of Heaven and Hell.*
[2] *Marriage of Heaven and Hell.*
[3] *Marriage of Heaven and Hell.*
[4] *First Defence*, p. 47.

matter which is of God; and the direct consequence of this theory is that God is most in the greatest men.

There is apparent under such utterances, in Blake and in Milton, a rationalizing spirit. This is shown most in the attitude towards dogma. Both poets accept dogma, but treat it as a symbol, as an empty vase into which they pour their own conceptions.

Blake gives a regularly rationalistic interpretation of religion in his address to the Christians:[1]

"I know of no other Christianity and of no other Gospel than the liberty both of body and mind to exercise the divine arts of Imagination. The Apostles knew of no other Gospel. What were all their spiritual gifts? What is the Divine Spirit? Is the Holy Ghost any other than an Intellectual Fountain? What is the Harvest of the Gospels and its Labours? What are the Treasures of Heaven which we are to lay up for ourselves, are they any other than Mental studies and performances? What are the gifts of the Gospel, are they not all mental gifts?—What is the Joy of Heaven but Improvement in the things of the Spirit? What are the pains of Hell but Ignorance, Bodily Lust, Idleness and devastation of the things of the

[1] *Jerusalem*, p. 77.

Spirit? To labour in knowledge is to build up Jerusalem; and to Despise Knowledge is to despise Jerusalem and her builders."

The Marriage of Heaven and Hell is even clearer in its rationalism:

"The Prophets Isaiah and Ezekiel dined with me, and I asked them how they dared so roundly assert that God spoke to them;

Isaiah answered: "I saw no God, nor heard any, in a finite organical perception; but my senses discover'd the infinite in everything, and as I was then persuaded, and remain confirmed, that the voice of honest indignation is the voice of God, I cared not for consequences, but wrote."

In such passages, Blake gives us, not only his interpretation of Christian dogma, but a cue to his own meaning in his mythology.

As we have seen, while the mood was on him, in *The Marriage of Heaven and Hell*, he rationalized Milton's world for him: Satan being Passion, the Messiah Reason, God Destiny and the Holy Ghost Vacuum. And in its large lines, the scheme certainly corresponds to Milton's thought.

Christ is for Milton the Power from above which embodied itself in our intelligence, for the triumph of Reason over Passion:

"His prophetic function consists of two parts;

one external, namely, the promulgation of divine truth, the other internal, to wit, the illumination of the understanding."[1]

And: "to restore man to the use of his natural faculties as regards the power to form right judgment and to exercise free will."[2]

Thus: "Believers are said to be engrafted in Christ"—"that is, partakers of Christ,"—"members of Christ's body."[3]

This interpretation runs through the whole of *Paradise Lost*, from the start:

> Till one Greater Man
> Restore us, and regain the blissful seat[4]

whereas, of course, the material Paradise was never regained, but, as Adam is told at the end:

> A Paradise within thee, happier far.[5]

Hence this explanation of the Almighty, which is historically quite impossible, since the Father gives it at the beginning of time, and yet places himself above all time, showing that the drama is

[1] *Treatise of Christian Doctrine*, p. 299.
[2] *T.C.D.*, p. 327.
[3] *T.C.D.*, p. 342 and 363.
[4] *Paradise Lost*, I, 4.
[5] *Paradise Lost*, XII, 586.

to take place within each human soul, even at the present moment:

> So heavenly love shall outdo hellish hate,
> Giving to death and dying to redeem,
> So dearly to redeem what hellish hate
> So easily destroyed, AND STILL DESTROYS
> In those who, when they may, accept not grace.[1]

Thus Milton, though a believer in the real historical facts of dogma, saw behind them a deeper meaning, following the Augustinian method:
"Those allegorical explanations are very good, provided one believe at the same time in the exactitude of the historical narrative."[2]
And this theory of Augustine and practice of Milton, Blake developed into his conception of the "double vision": accepting the facts of life as real, yet seeing behind them a deeper and larger reality:

> For double the vision my eyes do see
> And a double vision is always with me:
>   —in my double sight
> 'Twas outward a sun, inward Los in his might.

But Blake never can stop within any limits:

---

[1] *Paradise Lost*, III, 298.
[2] *City of God*, XIII, 21.

Los himself is the Prophetic spirit; and this is a "third Vision"; and even the Prophetic Spirit is an image of Something greater and more mysterious: probably a Function of the Eternal Man the Universal God—in the end perhaps simply a Faculty of the Human Mind. For, Blake says:

> Now I a fourfold vision see
> And a fourfold vision is given to me;
> 'Tis fourfold in my supreme delight,
> And threefold in soft Beulah's night
> And twofold always—May God us keep
> From single vision, and Newton's sleep.[1]

Thus Blake kindly gives to one of his friends a key which tempts us to try and explain his mythology. But in the end, he is only adopting the principle of interpretation used by Augustine and Milton: his ultimate "vision," when we can get to it, is generally something simple, and rational.

One reason of these complications is the deep need of the poetical genius of Blake and Milton for mythical thought. Bare abstract ideas do not satisfy them. The two poets want ideas to live, and to be clothed, not in mere symbols, but in existing Beings, Powers who walked the earth

[1] Letter to Butts. Sampson, p. 188–189.

like Christ—who was not only Jesus, but Intelligence in all men; Powers who inhabited mysterious worlds more real than ours, like Los and Urizen. Milton clung to his faith for the same reason that Blake believed in his Visions: both fully aware of the play of abstract ideas behind the vision, both intensely desirous that the abstract ideas should be real, active and powerfully living.

For both poets, their Figures were not mere allegories, or poetical personifications of psychological faculties, but supernatural conscious beings, realities. Those Beings were represented in us, men, by the quality in us which was their essence: For Milton, our Intelligence was Christ in us; for Blake, it was Urizen, our Feeling being Luvah. But Christ and Urizen and Luvah lived outside us as well as in those parts of us which were parts of Them; each of Them living partly in each particular man. Thus they united belief in the letter of religion—when it suited them—with the utmost possibilities of rationalism.

The theories of Blake, being developed, and applied, on a much larger scale, help us here to realize the state of mind of Milton. And in this similar way the two poets approached the Bible.

Both, as far as we can judge, adhered to the letter of the Bible to the end, and held it as their dearest possession and the most solid support of all their thought. Both had the power to write Biblical stuff, owing to their intimate communion with the Holy Book. Both used the Letter for the justification of the wildest heresies, and both occasionally by sheer force of intuition, discovered in the Bible, meanings which modern scholarship has revealed there only in the last century.

Milton wrote :

"We possess, as it were, a twofold Scripture, one external, which is the written word, and one internal, which is the Holy Spirit—that which is internal, and the peculiar possession of each believer is far superior to all, namely, the Spirit itself."[1]

"On the authority of Scripture itself, everything is to be referred finally to the Spirit, and the unwritten word."[2]

And therefore Milton used the Bible against all comers, chiefly against all orthodox theologians, to make a case of Arianism, materialism, pantheism, Arminianism, soul-mortalism, divorce, and polygamy : the *Treatise of Christian Doctrine* is a regular army of Biblical texts, marching under Milton's generalship to overcome all the tenets of ortho-

[1] *Treatise of Christian Doctrine*, p. 447.
[2] *T.C.D.*, p. 450.

doxy; and woe betide all texts which refuse to
march.

Milton might have said, as Blake, to his adversary:

> Both read the Bible day and night
> But thou read'st black when I read white.

For Blake has left us the immortal masterpiece
of that method of controversy, in his *Everlasting
Gospel*, where the whole of Christian morality is
shattered and ruined by the example of Jesus.

> The Vision of Christ that thou doest see
> Is my vision's greatest enemy.
> .   .   .   .
> Was Jesus gentle, or did He
> Give any marks of gentility?
> .   .   .   .
> Was Jesus humble? or did He
> Give any proofs of humility?

And so on to the bitter end:

> I am sure this Jesus will not do
> Either for Englishman or Jew.

Thus do those two astonishing compeers in
belief, believe.

Crabb Robinson reports of Blake:

"In connection with the assertion that the Bible is the Word of God and all truth is to be found in it—he qualified, and, as the orthodox would say, utterly nullified all he said by declaring that he understood the Bible in a spiritual sense."[1]

In the same way Milton had sung of

> Those records pure,
> Though not but by the Spirit understood.[2]

Indeed, both Milton and Blake might be regarded as powerful attempts of the English religious mind to get rid of the dogmatic orthodox forms of Christianity, by rationalizing them as much as possible, by interpreting what they kept, by adding to them when their thought needed it. Both were helped in their efforts by what they knew or guessed of the Jewish Cabala and of various occultist or oriental systems.[3] It might be said further that the attempt succeeded fully in Shelley, who has much in common with both, in his spirit of liberty and power of vision, and who stood further away from the forms of Christianity, although he also kept to the spirit.

---

[1] Crabb Robinson (Symons), p. 301.
[2] *Paradise Lost*, XII, 513.
[3] See on this: Saurat. *Milton, Man and Thinker. Blake and Modern Thought.*

Both Blake and Milton had the faith necessary to mythical poets; but Blake created, while Milton received and only interpreted; because Blake was following desire and Milton reason.

Both had the same need of reality; hence Milton's reason drove him into politics, towards practical reality, communion in effort with other men; Blake's desire drew him into mysticism, towards visionary reality, separating him from his fellow-men, because Milton's reason bade him try to mend this world; and Blake's desire attempted to create another.

It has been said often that reason unites men whereas feeling divides them. Milton was essentially social, delighting in the intellectual companionship of his contemporaries, and of all the great minds of the world's history. Blake was essentially solitary, finding no companion in his own time, and contemning fiercely most of the thinkers and artists he knew of, from Homer to Voltaire and Rembrandt.

They were brothers in the mind and in the heart, but Blake followed Desire and Milton followed Reason.

Therefore also, in his metaphysics, Blake had not the clarity and precision of Milton: Blake never clearly and methodically thought out a system of the universe, as Milton did in his *Treatise of Doctrine*. Feeling being cultivated in him rather than intelligence, his theories were built in a ramshackle manner upon intuitions and visions: but this is not always an inferiority, and sometimes it seems to us that the less logical thinker is also the more profound.

II.   METAPHYSICS

(a) God

There is in Milton a tendency to separate God from this world; to make Him higher, more incomprehensible to man:

> Fountain of Light, thyself invisible.[1]

The God of Milton is totally non-manifested. The poet centres on the Son all the usual ideas applicable to God, and makes God himself, above this secondary creative God, a Being infinitely greater, remoter, more inaccessible: the Sum Total of Being, of which the created universe is but a small part.

The longest chapter of the *Treatise of Christian Doctrine*[2] is devoted to the distinction between the Father and the Son:

[1] *Paradise Lost*, III, 376.
[2] Chapter V.

God is uncreated, infinite, unknowable;

The Son is created, finite, known by his acts.

"The Son was begotten—within the limits of time."[1]

He is finite : otherwise

"There would be two infinite Gods—which no man in his senses will admit."[2]

The Son is "The Word," the manifestation of God:

"Therefore the Word was audible. But God, as he cannot be seen, so neither can he be heard."[3]

"To be God—and to be from God—to be the one invisible God, and to be the only-begotten and visible, are things so different that they cannot be predicated of one and the same essence."[4]

This God cannot manifest himself; therefore he cannot create the World, Creation being manifestation. God, by his will, created the Son but God did not create the World: the Son is the Creator: "by whom afterwards all other things were made."[5]

The Son says to God:

> Father Eternal, thine is to decree,
> Mine both in heav'n and earth to do thy will.[6]

[1] *T. C. D.*, p. 84.   [2] *T. C. D.*, p. 85.
[3] *T. C. D.*, p. 109.   [4] *T. C. D.*, p. 143.
[5] *T. C. D.*, p. 81.   [6] *Paradise Lost*, X, 68.

Therefore, throughout the seventh book of *Paradise Lost* the Son creates the World: God is omnipresent, but inactive, and to him the Son returns:

> The Filial Power arrived, and sat him down
> With His great Father; for He also went
> Invisible, yet stayed, such privilege
> Has omnipresence.[1]

Blake accentuated this tendency of Milton to make God unknowable and inconceivable. In his Prophecies, he hardly speaks of God. God is unknown, even by the Eternals, and in Him are the ultimate secrets of Life:

Four mighty ones are in every Man: a perfect Unity
Cannot exist but from the Universal Brotherhood of
    Eden,
The Universal Man—
What are the Natures of those living creatures the
    Heavenly Father only
Knoweth: no Individual knoweth, nor can know in
    all Eternity.[2]

Just as in Milton the Son was the only Actor, so in Blake the Eternals and the Zoas, secondary Powers, are the only active ones.

[1] *Paradise Lost*, VII, 587.
[2] *Vala*, night 1, l. 4-8.

The Heavenly Father is only occasionally referred to, the New Born Man, that is, Perfect Man in his hour of regeneration being His Image:

Man liveth not by self alone, but in his brother's face
Each shall behold the Eternal Father and love and joy
    abound.

So spoke the Eternal—They embraced the new-born
    man.
Calling him Brother, image of the Eternal Father.[1]

So evidently the aim of this whole world is to realize that Image of the Eternal Father. But the Eternal Father is not the Creator.

Blake has an utterly different tale of creation to tell.

(b) Pantheism and Monism

Blake places the Fall at the very origin of things: this world was only created by the Zoas, specially by Urizen, as a result of the Fall. The event is described at length in *The First Book of Urizen:* from it come the present blindness of man, enclosed within his "senses five," the instauration of law, everything evil.

This world is in itself evil:

"Nature is the work of the Devil."[2]

[1] *Vala*, IX, 636.
[2] Crabb Robinson, Symons, p. 265.

Yet through it the will of God appears, leading the world towards salvation, and the Eternals are only performing that supreme Will. Just as in Milton the will of God is in Hell, whence the archfiend never

> Had risen or heaved his head, but that the will
> And high permission of high-ruling Heaven
> Left him at large to his own dark designs[1]—,

perhaps, as Beelzebub expresses it, in order to

> Do him mightier service, as his thralls
> By right of War, whate'er His business be
> Here in the heart of hell to work in fire,
> Or do his errands in the gloomy deep[2];

so in Blake God is everywhere:

God is within, and without; he is even in the depths of
    of Hell—[3]
And Los said: I behold the finger of God in terrors!
            —I saw the finger of God go forth,
—Giving a body to Falsehood that it may be cast off
    for ever.[4]

We have here a reason given us of creation, which is perhaps not so unMiltonic as it appears.

---

[1] *Paradise Lost*, I, 211.   [2] *Paradise Lost*, I, 148.
[3] *Jerusalem*, p. 12, l. 15.   [4] *Jerusalem*, p. 12.

God has created the world to cast off an evil part
of Himself. Milton has at least the elements of
this conception: he dared to write:

> Evil into the mind of God or man
> May come and go[1]

and in Milton's conception all creatures are but
parts of God, liberated from Him by his will that
they may fulfil their will, even as in the case of
Satan,

> —Left at large to his own dark designs
> That with reiterated crimes he might
> Heap on himself damnation.[2]

Was this not, as in Blake:

"Giving a body to Falsehood that it may be cast off
    for ever"?

And in both poets, this is but the dark side of a
sort of pantheism. God in Milton—God perhaps—
the Universal Man certainly, in Blake—are in
everything. The whole existence is One, and is
One Being.

Milton's God says, explaining at the same time
his omnipresence and the liberation of beings from

---

[1] *Paradise Lost*, V, 117.
[2] *Paradise Lost*, I, 213.

Himself, and the all-ruling power he yet keeps over them:

> Boundless the deep, because I am who fill
> Infinitude; nor vacuous the space.
> Though I uncircumscribed myself retire,
> And put not forth my goodness, which is free
> To act or not, Necessity and Chance
> Approach me not, and what I will is Fate.[1]

And no doubt, were Blake's God to reveal Himself, he might speak to the same effect.

As it is, in both poets we can trace the Universal Being in Man and in things.

Blake told the invaluable Crabb Robinson:

"We are all coexistent with God, members of the Divine body. We are all partakers of the Divine nature."[2]

A saying no less explicit than Milton's

> "All of us are of God."

In *The Marriage of Heaven and Hell*, Blake is in an explanatory mood, so we are told:

"God only acts and Is, in existing beings or Men"

and to a similar saying Blake adds:

> "for there is no other God."

[1] *Paradise Lost*, VII, 168.
[2] Crabb Robinson, p. 255.

The Everlasting Gospel, Blake's last word, is as explicit again: God says to man:

> Thou also dwellest in Eternity;
> Thou art a Man: God is no more.
> Thy own Humanity learn to adore,
> For that is my spirit of Life.

Milton went farther, and declared that matter itself was originally "from God," and that in matter the divine force moves upwards through the whole creation. God—the Son—is at once the Creator and the Creation which he drew from Himself:

"Matter—must have originated from God at some particular point of time;—There remains but one solution of the difficulty—namely, that all things are of God."[1]

"It is an argument of supreme power and goodness, that such diversified, multiform and inexhaustible virtue should exist and be substantially inherent in God—and not remain dormant within the Deity, but should be difused and extended."[2]

This is Milton's pantheism:

> O Adam, one Almighty is, from whom
> All things proceed, and up to Him return—
>   —one first matter all,

[1] *T. C. D.,* p. 178.   [2] *T. C. D.,* p. 179.

Indued with various forms, various degrees
Of substance, and in things that live, of life.[1]

Milton makes no difference of essence between
all created beings. And Blake echoes the belief:

For everything that lives is holy[2]

since, in Milton's words, "all things are of God."
Blake has his pantheism also, even though his
"God" be called "Man":

And as the seed waits eagerly watching for its flower
and fruit,
Anxious its little soul looks out into the clear expanse
To see if hungry winds are abroad with their invisible
array,
So Man looks out in tree and herb and fish and bird
and beast,
Collecting up the scattered portions of his immortal
body
Into the elemental forms of everything that grows.[3]

—Wherever a grass grows
Or a leaf buds, the Eternal Man is seen, is heard, is
felt
And all his sorrows, till he re-assumes his ancient
Bliss.[4]

---

[1] *Paradise Lost*, V, 468.   [3] *A Song of Liberty* in fine.
[2] *Vala*, VIII, 550, 573.   [4] *Vala*, I, 20.

And "Tharmas" who is instinctive life, the "Parent Power" says:

> The body of man is given to me—
> For still it surges forth in fish and monsters of the deeps
> And in these monstrous forms I live an eternal woe.[1]

For Blake's pantheism is black, owing to his evil idea of nature; whereas Milton rejoices in nature and the omnipresence of his God.

For both, the first consequence of this pantheism is monism or materialism. Since there is no difference between man and beast, even between man and things it can be said either that man has no soul, or that there is no difference between soul and body.

Milton writes in the Treatise:

"God infused the breath of life into other living beings.—Every living thing receives animation from one and the same source of life and breath."[2]

Hence God's words in *Paradise Lost:*

> And God said: Let the waters generate
> Reptile with spawn abundant, living soul
>
> .   .   .   .
>
> Let the earth bring forth soul living in her kind.[3]

---

[1] *Vala*, VI, 60.   [2] *T. C. D.*, p. 188.
[3] *Paradise Lost*, VII, 387, 451.

Soul then was given to all. Therefore:

"Man is a living being, intrinsically and properly one and individual, not compound and separable, not, according to the common opinion, made up and framed of two distinct and different natures as soul and body."[1]

"That the spirit of man should be separate from the body, so as to have a perfect and intelligent existence independently of it—the doctrine is evidently at variance both with nature and reason. For the word "soul" (in the Bible) is applied to every kind of living being."[2]

Blake could not know those words of Milton when he wrote in *The Marriage of Heaven and Hell*:

"Man has no body distinct from his soul; for that call'd Body is a portion of Soul discern'd by the five Senses, the chief inlets of Soul in this age."

And if we like to call this idealism, Milton is then also such an idealist; he can be as metaphysical as Blake himself:

"Spirit being the more excellent substance, virtually and essentially contains within itself the inferior one, as the spiritual and rational faculty contains the corporeal, that is, the sentient and vegetative faculty."[3]

[1] *T. C. D.*, p. 188.   [2] *T. C. D.*, p. 189.
[3] *T. C. D.*, p. 181.

But then Milton would not have heard a word of disparagement of the body and matter, which Blake condemns on all occasions:

"For the original matter—is not to be looked upon as an evil or trivial thing, but as intrinsically good, and the chief productive stock of every subsequent good."[1]

Still, the two poets only disagree on this point of appreciation. Their doctrine remains similar: and both proceed to a next step of their Pantheism in agreement.

Everything is holy, a part of the One being, hence everything is immortal.

Milton says: "If all things are not only from God, but of God, no created thing can be finally annihilated."[2]

And Blake sings:

For everything exists and not one sigh nor smile nor
    tear,
One hair or particle of dust, not one can pass away.[3]

Death was brought into the world by the Fall: Hence Milton's allegory of Sin and Death, and his grand picture of Sin ushering Death into the Earth after the Fall:

[1] *T. C. D.*, p. 179.   [2] *T. C. D.*, p. 181.
[3] *Jerusalem*, p. 13, 66 and 14, 1.

> Both to destroy or unimmortal make
> All kinds.[1]

As for Blake, this very world is nothing but Death to him, and it is caused by the Fall; hence the necessity of dying in order to get out of it would not have existed but for the Fall.

Neither of the two poets makes any distinction between soul and body in the matter of death. Milton is argumentative and tries to show at length that the soul (if we needs must use the word)

"is subject to death, natural as well as violent."[2]

Blake serenely ignores the point, as is logical for him—as it ought to be for Milton—once the distinction between body and soul is suppressed.

So for both Death is only a passing accident, properly, as Milton explains, a sleep, from which we awake into God's real life:

"If it be true that there is no time without motion, which Aristotle illustrates by the example of those who were fabled to have slept in the temple of the heroes, and who, on awaking, imagined that the moment in which they awoke had succeeded without an interval to that in which

---

[1] *Paradise Lost*, X, 610.
[2] *T. C. D.*, p. 225 and chap. XIII.

they fell asleep; how much more must intervening time be annihilated to the departed, so that to them to die and to be with Christ will seem to take place at the same moment."[1]

Hence Milton has been called one of the "soul-sleepers." . . .

Blake extended the idea to this life itself: death in his system: he calls it "the sleep of Ulro" repeatedly; and, aptly enough, he makes Milton pray thus:

When will the Resurrection come to deliver the
    sleeping body
From corruptibility? O when, Lord Jesus, wilt Thou
    come?[2]

He seems to mean by corruptibility this mortal life of ours, and the deliverance which he calls Resurrection we should call Death. But whatever the complication of the meaning, there is the obvious identification of Death with Sleep, as a passing accident: and that is substantially Milton's idea.

[1] *T. C. D.*, p. 280.
[2] *Milton*, p. 12.

(c) Regeneration

In their idea of Regeneration both poets are again at one: for both, the Regenerate Man becomes a member of Christ. From the Communion of all the Elect, one aggregate being is formed, who is named Jesus; or, as it is sometimes expressed inversely, the Saviour incarnates himself in the soul of all the Elect. A sort of special pantheism appears in both poets for the benefit of the Regenerate: they become members of Christ and of one another.

One difference comes out here: this pantheism is limited for Milton, while Blake really admits every being to his Regeneration: there are no damned in his system.

A new creation is necessary to bring man to the regenerate Life. This creation takes place through Christ's coming into us "to create afresh, as it were, the inward man, and infuse from above new and supernatural faculties into the minds of the renovated. This is called regeneration, and the regenerate are said to be engrafted in Christ."[1]

That is the "Greater Man" which is to restore us the "Paradise within," not from the outside, but because we shall be parts of Him.

[1] *T. C. D.*, p. 327–328.

God explains to Christ that he shall save

> them who renounce
> Their own both righteous and unrighteous deeds,
> And live in thee transplanted, and in thee
> Receive new life.[1]

Thus Blake insists on the necessity of putting "Selfhood" aside:

> however high
> Our palaces and cities, and however fruitful are our
> fields,
> In Selfhood we are nothing, but fade away into
> morning's breath.
> Our mildness is nothing: the greatest mildness we can
> use
> Is incapable and nothing; none but the Lamb of God
> can heal
> This dread disease, none but Jesus: O Lord, descend
> and Save.[2]

And Jesus descends into us, as in Milton, that we may live:

> Albion said: O Lord what can I do my Selfhood cruel
> Marches against thee—

[1] *Paradise Lost*, III, 291.
[2] *Jerusalem*, p. 45, l. 12.

I behold the visions of my deadly Sleep of Six
    Thousand years,
Dazzling around my skirts like a Serpent of precious
    stones and gold:
I know it is my Self: O my divine Creator and
    Redeemer.

Jesus replied: Fear not, Albion: unless I die thou canst
    not live:
But if I die I shall arise again and thou with me.
This is Friendship and Brotherhood: without it Man
    is not.[1]

"Die" means for Blake come into this world: as

"God becomes as we are, that we may be as he is."[2]

that is to say: God descends among us, into us, in
order to raise us to Him:

And if God dieth not for Man and giveth not Himself
Eternally for Man, Man could not exist.[3]

And the Saviour speaks at the beginning of
Jerusalem:

[1] *Jerusalem*, p. 96.
[2] Tract: *There is no natural religion.*
[3] *Jerusalem*, p. 96.

I am not a God afar off, I am a brother and a friend
Within your bosoms I reside, and you reside in me:
Lo! We are One; forgiving all Evil: Not seeking
    recompense
Ye are my members, O ye sleepers of Beulah, land of
    shades.[1]

This makes precise Milton's conception of the "Greater Man," and Blake seems bent on elucidation of that point:

We live as One Man: for contracting our infinite
    senses
We behold multitude: or expanding we behold as
    One.
As one man the Universal Family: and that One
    Man
We call Jesus the Christ: and he in us, and we in him
Live in perfect harmony in Eden the Land of Life.[2]

              Till one Greater Man
    Restore us, and regain the blissful seat

said Milton. And the lines of Blake are the best possible explanation of that concentrated and all too full text: the key to the meaning of much

---

[1] *Jerusalem*, p. 4.
[2] *Jerusalem*, p. 38.

of Milton's Christianity. If often Milton has helped us to understand Blake, at this ultimate and most essential point, Blake helps us to understand Milton.

CONCLUSION

We have seen that the systems of thought of Blake and Milton are both based on the idea of Liberty.

Blake never troubles to try and prove free-will; it is in his work a complete assumption; he believes in it as much as Milton, who devotes chapters of his Treatise and well-nigh cantos of his poem to the demonstration of it.

Yet both poets believe in a Presiding Spirit in the Universe. "God becomes as we are, that we may be as he is."

This is the best reason Blake can give us for the existence of this universe: really, the development of the Life of God: since we came from Him in the beginning.

And Milton's God has the same purpose; and keeps the same high hand over his creatures:

> Though I uncircumscribed myself retire
> And put not forth my goodness, which is free
> To act or not, Necessity and Chance
> Approach me not, and what I will is Fate.

As Blake says, Milton's God is "Eternal Destiny"; and His aim is the ultimate glory of the Communion of all the Elect with Him.

In Blake the similar end of all things is the glorious final Regeneration of all beings.

But Blake starting from Milton's data: God-Destiny, Son-Reason; Satan-Passion; and adding to them the other Miltonic couple: Son-Creation, was logical with himself: as Reason was evil for him, the Creation of the Son, who was Reason, was evil: "a world stolen from the Abyss." This life Blake called death. The creation was to him a Fall, while to Milton it was a progress: a step in the fulfilment of the Eternal Plan.

Therefore with Milton the general aim and plan of Life is clearer: we do not see in Blake why God permitted all the tremendous tumult.

In reality, the same principle created the world for both: free-will, the necessity that each being should express its possibilities. Milton clearly added to that idea the belief that yet God kept the leadership, saying:

What I will is Fate—
—Though I uncircumscribed myself retire,

and liberate independent beings.

Blake is troubled before the World: he feels the terror and the evil more deeply than Milton: he is less sure of the hand of God behind. Yet in the end, for him also the Final Existence is all the grander because of the struggles.

Thus and with those differences, the two schemes of life run parallel in the work of the two poets.

Thus, starting from similarity of character and difference of purpose, expressed through ethics, psychology and religion, culminates in the highest flights of poetical metaphysics the strange brotherhood of the two poets' souls,

"l'ombre de l'une mêlée à la lumière de l'autre."[1]

[1] "The gloom of the one mingled with the light of the other" (Victor Hugo, *Quatre-vingt-treize*, in fine).